SOMETHING

NEEDS

TO

CHANGE

A Call to Make Your Life Count
in a World of Urgent Need

DAVID PLATT

LifeWay Press®
Nashville, Tennessee

ABOUT THE AUTHOR

DAVID PLATT serves as the pastor of McLean Bible Church in metro Washington, D.C. He's the founder and president of Radical (Inc.), a global ministry and giving platform whose purpose is to serve the church and spread the gospel on the front lines of urgent need around the world. Resources from David Platt and Radical can be found at radical.net.

David is the author of several books, including *Radical, Radical Together, Follow Me, Counter Culture,* and *Something Needs to Change,* as well as the following volumes in the Christ-Centered Exposition Commentary series: *Exalting Jesus in Matthew, Exalting Jesus in James, Exalting Jesus in 1 & 2 Timothy and Titus,* and *Exalting Jesus in Galatians.*

David Platt received his PhD from New Orleans Baptist Theological Seminary. He lives in the metro Washington, D.C., area with his wife and their children.

INTRODUCTION

Not long ago the Lord turned my life upside down on a trek through the Himalayan trails.

As a pastor, I travel overseas three or four times a year, and this trip started just like any other. I was taking a small group of other pastors with me to explore opportunities for ministry partnerships among men, women, and children in remote mountain regions. We flew to a major city, where we rested for a night, and then we boarded a helicopter that would take us twelve thousand feet higher than the rest of the world. We landed on a small plateau of land surrounded by majestic mountaintops, stepped out of the helicopter with small bags on our backs, and began a trek out of the mountains that would take us six days to hike.

By the end of that adventure, I was sitting stunned in an airport, saying to the pastors around me, "I don't know what all of this means, but I know this. Something needs to change. Something is going to change." Little did I know what that change would mean for my life.

Now, a couple of years removed from that trek through those Himalayan trails, I don't believe what I saw, smelled, felt, and experienced was just for me. And I don't think that trip was intended to change the trajectory of my life alone. The questions I found myself wrestling with on those freezing nights in the mountains are questions I'm convinced we all need to wrestle with. Where is God amid suffering in this world? Why was I born into relative comfort, while so many men, women, and children are born into desperate poverty? Surely I have a responsibility to use the resources I have, but what am I supposed to do? What's my duty in this world?

This Bible study isn't simply an attempt to give you my answers to these questions. These are questions we all need to ask, and I hope this Bible-study experience will help you do that. I want to take readers on a journey with me through remote Himalayan trails to wrestle with realities we all need to wrestle with and to consider how these realities in the world around us, in light of God's Word to us, need to shape our lives, our families, and our churches. I want to invite other followers of Jesus to come to the point where we say together, "Something needs to change. Something is going to change."

HOW TO USE THIS STUDY

This Bible-study book provides eight weeks of content for group and personal study.

GROUP SESSIONS

Regardless of what day of the week your group meets, each session of content begins with the group session. Each group session uses the following format to facilitate simple yet meaningful interaction among group members and with the truths of God's Word presented in this study.

START

This page includes questions to get the conversation started and to introduce the video teaching.

DISCUSS

This page includes questions and statements that guide the group to respond to David's video teaching and to explore relevant Bible passages.

PARTICIPANT GUIDE

Each session includes a participant guide to help group members follow along with the video teaching. Additionally, the second page of the participant guide features action steps and questions designed to lead group members to think more deeply about what God is teaching them through this study.

PERSONAL STUDY

REFLECTIONS

Each session of personal study begins with an excerpt from the book *Something Needs to Change,* in which David reflects on his trip to the Himalayas.

PERSONAL STUDY

Each session provides three personal Bible studies, using the REAP method. Each personal study includes a passage from the Gospel of Luke, along with commentary and questions to help participants under-stand the Bible and apply its teaching to their lives.

THE REAP METHOD

Each session features three personal Bible studies, using the REAP method.

READ

Read the passage of Scripture asking the Holy Spirit to give you encouragement, direction, and correction (see 2 Tim. 3:16). Highlight verses and phrases that stand out to you as particularly important.

EXAMINE

Spend time reflecting on and writing about the Scriptures you've read. This section will help you respond to those Scriptures by thinking through the following questions.

- What's occurring in the passage?
- What's the big theme or takeaway from this passage?
- Why did the biblical author include this passage?
- What does this passage teach you about God? About people? About Jesus? About the necessity of faith? About the urgency of eternity?

APPLY

After examining the passage, apply the text to your life. The questions in this section will help you consider ways the Scripture you've read that day changes the way you live.

PRAY

Pray and ask God to change your heart and your life, based on your study of God's Word.

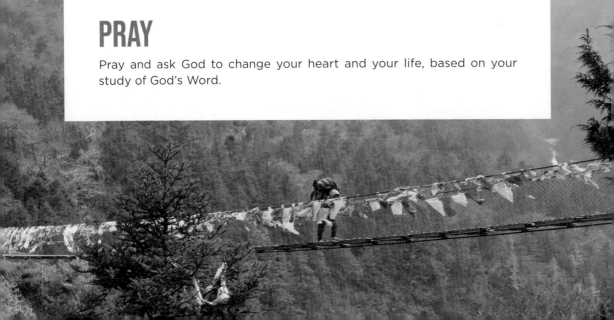

TIPS **FOR LEADING A SMALL GROUP**

Follow these guidelines to prepare for each group session.

PRAYERFULLY PREPARE

REVIEW. Review each session's material and group questions ahead of time.

PRAY. Intentionally pray for each person in the group.

Ask the Holy Spirit to work through you and the group discussion as you point to Jesus through God's Word.

MINIMIZE DISTRACTIONS

Create an environment that's conducive to small-group discussion. Plan ahead by considering details like seating, temperature, lighting, and general cleanliness.

At best, thoughtfulness and hospitality show guests and group members they're welcome and valued in whatever environment you choose to gather. Do everything in your ability to help people focus on what's most important: connecting with God, with the Bible, and with one another.

ENCOURAGE DISCUSSION

A good small-group experience has the following characteristics.

INCLUDE OTHERS. Your goal is to foster a community in which people are welcome just as they are but are encouraged to grow spiritually. An inexpensive way to make first-time guests feel welcome or to invite someone to get involved is to give them their own copies of this Bible-study book.

EVERYONE PARTICIPATES. Encourage everyone to ask questions, share responses, or read aloud.

NO ONE DOMINATES—NOT EVEN THE LEADER. Be sure that your time speaking as a leader takes up less than half of your time together as a group. Politely guide discussion if anyone dominates.

DON'T RUSH THROUGH QUESTIONS. Don't feel that a moment of silence is a bad thing. People often need time to think about their responses to questions they've just heard or to gain courage to share what God is stirring in their hearts.

INPUT IS AFFIRMED AND FOLLOWED UP. Make sure you point out something true or helpful in a response. Don't just move on. Build community with follow-up questions, asking how other people have had similar experiences or how a truth has shaped their understanding of God and the Scripture you're studying. People are less likely to speak up if they fear that you don't actually want to hear their answers or that you're looking for only a certain answer.

GOD AND HIS WORD ARE CENTRAL. Opinions and experiences can be helpful, but God has given us the truth. Trust God's Word to be the authority and God's Spirit to work in people's lives. You can't change anyone, but God can. Continually point people to the Word and to active steps of faith.

KEEP CONNECTING

Think of ways to connect with group members during the week. Participation during the group session always improves when members spend time connecting with one another outside the group sessions. The more people are comfortable with and involved in one another's lives, the more they'll look forward to being together. When people move beyond being friendly to truly being friends who form a community, they come to each session eager to engage instead of merely attending.

PRAY FOR THE PEOPLES OF THE HIMALAYAS

In some parts of the world, following Jesus is a dangerous pursuit. The trek described in this Bible study details events seen and heard through multiple trips on Himalayan trails, where the gospel isn't always welcome. Everything and everyone described in this study is real, but for security reasons, key names, places, times, and other details have been altered to protect the people involved.

The people groups described here are emblematic of the people groups who live in the mountains.

GENERAL STATISTICS

The gospel has made very little progress in the Himalayas, not only because these people are hard to reach but also because these mountain ranges have historically been a stronghold of Buddhism, particularly Tibetan Buddhism. Many important Buddhist monasteries and religious sites are located in the Himalayas.

Less than half of 1 percent of the villagers in the Himalayas know Jesus. Many have never even heard the name Jesus.

More than 98 percent of the inhabitants of the Himalayas would describe themselves as Buddhist. However, in addition to Buddhism, their religious beliefs contain a mixture of magic, divination, demon worship, and sacrifices.

Tibetan Buddhists are considered unreached. According to the Joshua Project, "An unreached or least-reached people is a people group among which there is no indigenous community of believing Christians with adequate numbers and resources to evangelize this people group without outside assistance."[1]

Many dialects spoken by Tibetan Buddhists have access to a full translation of the Scriptures.

SPECIFIC PRAYERS

- Ask God to raise up committed teams of people to pray for the harvest in the Himalayas.
- Pray that God will raise up laborers for the harvest (see Luke 10:2).
- Ask God to encourage and protect the few known Christians in mountain villages.
- Pray that these believers will have opportunities to share Christ with their own people.
- Ask God to open the hearts of government leaders to allow Christians to gather for worship.
- Pray that God will turn Buddhists from the fear and bondage of their religion to salvation in Christ.
- Ask the Lord to raise up strong local churches in the mountains.
- Ask that God will use this study to challenge believers to give their lives for the sake of His glory among all the peoples of the world.

1. Joshua Project, accessed July 9, 2019, https://joshuaproject.net/help/definitions.

01

Repentance

START

Welcome to session 1 of Something Needs to Change. *Use these questions to begin the conversation.*

Where's the farthest place you've ever traveled from home?

Have you ever gone on a mission trip to another country? What was that experience like?

Something Needs to Change follows Pastor David Platt on a journey through remote Himalayan villages. Of an estimated nine million people in the region where the videos for this Bible study were filmed, there are only one hundred followers of Jesus. Most people in this region have never heard the name of Jesus. Although it would be amazing for our group to go on the trek David took, the hope of this Bible study is to give us a glimpse into a region of the world filled with urgent physical and spiritual need. As we do, let's pray that the Spirit of God will challenge us and reveal areas of our lives that need to change.

Before we begin, have someone pray for our study, asking God to work and show us what needs to change in our own lives.

After praying watch the video, "Day 1: Repentance." Encourage group members to follow along, using the participant guide on pages 173–74 or at LifeWay.com/ SomethingNeedstoChange.

To access video sessions, subscribe to SmallGroup.com or visit LifeWay.com/SomethingNeedstoChange.

DISCUSS

Use these questions to discuss the video teaching in your group.

David said every time he visits the region of the world featured in these videos, he's forced to ask hard questions. What kinds of experiences caused a similar paradigm shift in your life?

David mentioned that the Word of God shaped what he saw in the mountains. Why should we test our experience against the Word of God?

In His sovereignty God uses moments in our lives to shape us into the image of His Son. Visiting places outside our culture and comfort zone alerts us to physical and spiritual needs in a way few other experiences can. However, as helpful as those experiences are, they must be tested against the Word of God.

Refer to Luke 3:1-18 for the following questions.

John the Baptist proclaimed a message of repentance (see v. 3). What does it mean to repent? Why is true repentance different from religious activity?

How do you typically respond to the needs you encounter in the world?

John prepared the way for Jesus by calling people to repent of their sins. Repentance is different from religious activity, which simply changes our behavior. Repentance results in a transformed heart, which changes our thoughts, motivations, and actions. John was calling the crowds to respond to God's grace with true, life-changing repentance (see vv. 11-14). Likewise, when confronted with needs, we can't do nothing.

Look again at verses 9 and 17. How did John describe the coming judgment of Christ? What does this kind of language teach us?

How does the reality of impending judgment increase
the urgency to take the gospel to the ends of the earth?

The images of judgment in these passages are stark and visceral. John's
metaphors highlight what's at stake in our mission to the world. The
nine million people around the Himalayas and billions around the globe
will one day stand before God as Judge. And the only way they can be
saved on that day is through faith in Jesus. Through Jesus, the call to
repent is also a message of hope.

Look again at verses 3-6. How does the world change when
God's salvation spreads?

How have you seen the world change as people encounter
and believe the gospel message?

Before John painted a picture of judgment, he offered promises of
coming grace. In verses 4-6 we see a total reversal of the order of the
world. The Lord is preparing a path for all people to know Him. As
obstacles are removed, "everyone will see the salvation of God" (v. 6).
As the gospel moves forward, the world changes, across the street and
around the world.

PRAYER

*God, thank You for saving us and calling us to live for the spread
of Your gospel and glory in the world. Help us identify specific
areas into which You're calling us. Lead us to be open to Your
calling in our lives.*

**As you close, remind the group to complete the three personal
studies that follow. Encourage them to spend time thinking about
the suggestions for getting involved, located on the back of the
participant guide.**

Prepare the way for the Lord;
make his paths straight!
Every valley will be filled,
and every mountain
and hill will be made low;
the crooked will become straight,
the rough ways smooth,
AND EVERYONE
WILL SEE THE
SALVATION OF GOD.

LUKE 3:4-6

Excited but Tired

Thirty hours in coach on an airplane to the Himalayas wears you out.

We gather our carry-ons, and as we exit the jetway, new sights, smells, and sounds bombard our senses. Almost everyone around us is speaking a different language. Many of the women are wearing long, casual, colorful outfits with a head covering. Some of the men sport long, baggy, double-breasted shirts over matching pants. The airport restaurants give off a uniquely pungent aroma of spice and seasoning. Although we're exhausted, we quickly realize we're not in Kansas anymore.

Somewhat disoriented anyway, we feel our anxiety rise because we're not certain what to do or where to go. The airport signs are puzzling, written in another language and sometimes translated into English in ways that don't quite make sense.

When in doubt, go with the herd, so we hoist our packs and follow our fellow passengers toward customs. With groans we see a long line that's scarcely moving. As we creep along, we exchange glances of frustration. There's nothing to do but stand and shuffle.

After an hour-long wait, which provides us with plenty of time to stretch our legs, we hand our passports to an agent, who glances at each of our photos and then at our faces before verifying the validity of our visas.

"Why are you visiting our country"? he asks.

"We want to trek through the mountains," I answer.

He nods, stamps each passport, and waves us through.

Because we're carrying everything we need in our backpacks, there's no other baggage to retrieve.

Our friend Aaron picks us up, and we make our way to the guesthouse where we'll be staying for the night. In this large Asian city, even though it's several hours after sundown, the streets are clogged with traffic—every imaginable type of two-, three-, and four-wheeled vehicle, from pedal bikes to rickshaws to scooters to cars to buses to semitrucks. Chaos!

I notice my eyes slightly stinging from the pollution, with clouds of exhaust and dust rising from semipaved streets. Some of the residents riding two-wheelers are wearing surgical masks to screen out some of the dirty air. After an hour in the hectic traffic, we arrive at the guesthouse—ah, at last an opportunity to stretch out and sleep.

I make my way to my guesthouse room, a quaint setup with a single bed and a side table. A small window opens to the outside, letting a cool breeze gently blow into the room. With the soft wind comes steady noise from the street as men and women, cars and motorcycles continue in what seems like never-ending activity.

> I began writing reflections on what God was teaching me in His Word. ... Those reflections would inevitably turn into prayers of praise and thanks to Him, petitions for my life, and intercession for others.

As I climb into bed, I pull my journal from my pack. When I was younger, a mentor encouraged me to journal my experiences with God. I began writing reflections on what God was teaching me in His Word and on ways I saw Him working in my life and in the world around me. Those reflections would inevitably turn into prayers of praise and thanks to Him, petitions for my life, and intercession for others. I can't say I've journaled every day since that time, but I've done so off and on for many years and almost every day in recent years. Even though I can barely hold my eyes open, I know I must write about this experience.

PERSONAL STUDY 1

INTRODUCTION TO LUKE

All life change begins with God's Word. The single most important habit a Christian can develop is regularly feasting on the Scriptures. Throughout this study we'll work through the Gospel of Luke. In the Scriptures you see God's character revealed through His Word and His Son. As you encounter the living God, you begin to see what needs to change in your life.

■ THE AUTHOR

LUKE

Luke was a doctor, researcher, and companion of Paul. He was the author of the two volumes of Luke and Acts, which tell the story of Jesus and the early church. He was likely a Gentile.

■ PURPOSE

The Gospel of Luke is a carefully researched (see 1:3), selective presentation of the person and life of Jesus Christ, designed to strengthen the faith of believers (see 1:3-4) and to challenge the misconceptions of unbelievers, especially those from a Greek background. Its portrait of Jesus is well balanced, skillfully emphasizing His divinity and perfect humanity.

Three important themes in Luke's Gospel are the prayers of Jesus, the work of the Holy Spirit, and God's concern for the oppressed and the nations.

READ

Slowly and intentionally read the Scriptures.

READ LUKE 1:1-4.

LUKE 1:1-4

1 Many have undertaken to **compile a narrative** about the events that have been fulfilled among us, [2] just as the original **eyewitnesses** and servants of the word handed them down to us. [3] It also seemed good to me, since I have carefully investigated everything from the very first, to write to you in an orderly sequence, most honorable Theophilus, [4] so that you may know the certainty of the things about which you have been instructed.

■ COMPILE A NARRATIVE [V. 1]

One reason we know we can trust the Bible is the authenticity of the record. For example, Luke tells us he took the time to carefully interview many eyewitnesses of the life and ministry of Jesus.

When we pick up Luke's Gospel, we're reading a thorough account of Jesus' life that was researched and fact-checked, so to speak. We can trust what we read.

■ WORD STUDY

EYEWITNESSES [V. 2]

Verse 2 refers to eyewitnesses, an important concept for our understanding of Luke. The doctor took great care to compile a narrative of the life of Jesus Christ by interviewing eyewitnesses. The Gospel of Luke is a product of careful investigation. Luke's account is thoughtful and intentional, containing much original material not found in the other Gospel accounts.

EXAMINE

Gain a deeper appreciation for what the biblical text says.

Take a few moments to read Luke 1:1-4 again, circling all of the words Luke used to describe his Gospel.

LUKE 1:1-4

1 Many have undertaken to compile a narrative about the events that have been fulfilled among us, ² just as the original eyewitnesses and servants of the word handed them down to us. ³ It also seemed good to me, since I have carefully investigated everything from the very first, to write to you in an orderly sequence, most honorable Theophilus, ⁴ so that you may know the certainty of the things about which you have been instructed.

Why do these words seem particularly important? What was important to Luke in capturing the life of Jesus?

In verse 4 Luke said he wanted Theophilus, the recipient of Luke's writing, to have certainty. How do the Scriptures provide us with certainty?

Why is it important for us to be able to believe in the reliability of Scripture?

APPLY

Recognize that the Bible calls us to obedience and to respond to God with our lives.

Luke understood that the story of Jesus was so important that he had to share it. Do you feel an urgency to share the gospel with others? Why or why not?

Identify some barriers that keep you from sharing the gospel with others.

PRAY

Respond to God with praise, thanksgiving, confession, and obedience.

Record a prayer to God in light of today's reading. Begin by asking Him to give you a desire to share His Word among all nations.

PERSONAL STUDY 2

READ

Slowly and intentionally read the Scriptures.

READ LUKE 2:8-20.

Today we'll look at a passage of Scripture that's most often considered at Christmas. It's one of the most popular and memorable passages in Scripture for good reason: it's a great story. However, it's so much more. The shepherds' encounter with the angel has much to teach us about God's character and mission to the nations.

LUKE 2:8-11

8 In the same region, shepherds were staying out in the fields and keeping watch at night over their flock. 9 Then an angel of the Lord stood before them, and the glory of the Lord shone around them, and they were terrified. 10 But the angel said to them, "Don't be afraid, for look, I proclaim to you good news of great joy that will be for all the people: 11 Today in the city of David a **Savior** was born for you, who is the **Messiah**, the **Lord**.

■ TITLES OF JESUS [V. 11]

The angel of the Lord announced, "A Savior was born for you, who is the Messiah, the Lord" (v. 11). These three titles, which appear together nowhere else in Scripture, aren't incidental. They point to Jesus' identity.

JESUS IS SAVIOR

The one true God had broken into history to save His people from their sin. A Savior had been born. Jesus alone can save people from their sin. The rescue Luke wrote about has physical and spiritual dimensions.

JESUS IS MESSIAH

Christ is the Greek version of the Hebrew term *Messiah,* meaning "Anointed One." Jesus isn't a Deliverer; He's *the* Deliverer. He alone is the promised Anointed One.

JESUS IS LORD

The term *Lord* is used to describe Yahweh in the Greek translation of the Old Testament. This title refers to the absolute sovereignty Jesus possesses as the One who brings salvation.

■ NOTICE THE RESPONSES [VV. 15,19]

Pay close attention to the shepherds' and Mary's responses. The shepherds ran to tell the news. Mary turned over the thoughts in her heart, holding on to them for further contemplation. These verses make clear that Jesus demands a response. Both responses in this passage are correct; we're called to do both. The news that Jesus is Savior, Messiah, and Lord is to be shared and treasured. What we can't do is nothing.

LUKE 2:13-20

¹³ Suddenly there was a multitude of the heavenly host with the angel, praising God and saying:
¹⁴   Glory to God in the highest heaven,
        and peace on earth to people he favors!
¹⁵ When the angels had left them and returned to heaven, the shepherds said to one another, "Let's go straight to Bethlehem and see what has happened, which the Lord has made known to us."
¹⁶ They hurried off and found both Mary and Joseph, and the baby who was lying in the manger. ¹⁷ After seeing them, they reported the message they were told about this child, ¹⁸ and all who heard it were amazed at what the shepherds said to them. ¹⁹ But Mary was treasuring up all these things in her heart and meditating on them. ²⁰ The shepherds returned, glorifying and praising God for all the things they had seen and heard, which were just as they had been told.

■ CONTEXT

Notice that the news of Jesus' birth came to shepherds. You may have heard a sermon pointing out that shepherds were despised and downtrodden. This view is probably overstated. Luke wanted us to see that God revealed Himself to common people. The announcement of Jesus' birth didn't come to a king or the elite but to lowly, ordinary, hardworking shepherds. Luke's birth narrative shows us that Jesus came to be the Redeemer of all people.

EXAMINE

Gain a deeper appreciation for what the biblical text says.

Circle, underline, or highlight all of the places the shepherds and Mary responded to the news of Jesus.

LUKE 2:13-20

13 Suddenly there was a multitude of the heavenly host with the angel, praising God and saying:
14 Glory to God in the highest heaven,
and peace on earth to people he favors!
15 When the angels had left them and returned to heaven, the shepherds said to one another, "Let's go straight to Bethlehem and see what has happened, which the Lord has made known to us."
16 They hurried off and found both Mary and Joseph, and the baby who was lying in the manger. 17 After seeing them, they reported the message they were told about this child, 18 and all who heard it were amazed at what the shepherds said to them. 19 But Mary was treasuring up all these things in her heart and meditating on them. 20 The shepherds returned, glorifying and praising God for all the things they had seen and heard, which were just as they had been told.

Why does Jesus always merit a response of some kind?

What does this passage teach us about Jesus? What does it teach us about the necessity of faith?

APPLY

Recognize that the Bible calls us to obedience and to respond to God with our lives.

How are you responding to Jesus right now? After reading Luke 2, how do you plan to act?

Why does the gospel message compel us both to treasure its truths and to proclaim them to the world? How are you doing both?

PRAY

Respond to God with praise, thanksgiving, confession, and obedience.

Record a prayer to God in light of today's reading.

PERSONAL STUDY 3

READ

Slowly and intentionally read the Scriptures.

READ LUKE 3:1-18.

Most passages of Scripture have one key takeaway. Here the idea is repentance. Although this might not be a very popular word or thought in today's culture, it's thoroughly biblical. Repentance is necessary because our sin has separated us from God. We balk at the call to repent because it confronts our sinfulness and self-sufficiency. Repentance takes place only after we realize that we've been tainted by the stain of sin and that we need redemption.

LUKE 3:1-6

3 In the fifteenth year of the reign of Tiberius Caesar, while Pontius Pilate was governor of Judea, Herod was tetrarch of Galilee, his brother Philip tetrarch of the region of Iturea and Trachonitis, and Lysanias tetrarch of Abilene, ² during the high priesthood of Annas and Caiaphas, God's word came to John the son of Zechariah in the wilderness. ³ He went into all the vicinity of the Jordan, proclaiming a baptism of **repentance** for the forgiveness of sins, ⁴ as it is written in the book of the words of the prophet Isaiah:

> **A voice of one crying out in the wilderness:**
> **Prepare the way for the Lord;**
> **make his paths straight!**
> ⁵ **Every valley will be filled,**
> **and every mountain and hill will be made low;**
> **the crooked will become straight,**
> **the rough ways smooth,**
> ⁶ **and everyone will see the salvation of God.**

■ MAIN THEME

REPENTANCE [V. 3]

Repentance means we turn away from our sin and turn 180 degrees to God. All people have a sin problem that can be resolved only when they repent of their sin and believe the gospel of Jesus Christ (see Mark 1:14-15).

LUKE 3:7-18

[7] He then said to the crowds who came out to be baptized by him, "Brood of vipers! Who warned you to flee from the coming wrath? [8] Therefore produce fruit consistent with repentance. And don't start saying to yourselves, 'We have Abraham as our father,' for I tell you that God is able to raise up children for Abraham from these stones. [9] The ax is already at the root of the trees. Therefore, every tree that doesn't produce good fruit will be cut down and thrown into the fire."

[10] **"What then should we do?"** the crowds were asking him.

[11] He replied to them, "The one who has two shirts must share with someone who has none, and the one who has food must do the same."

[12] Tax collectors also came to be baptized, and they asked him, **"Teacher, what should we do?"**

[13] He told them, "Don't collect any more than what you have been authorized."

[14] Some soldiers also questioned him, **"What should we do?"**

He said to them, "Don't take money from anyone by force or false accusation, and be satisfied with your wages."

[15] Now the people were waiting expectantly, and all of them were questioning in their hearts whether John might be the Messiah. [16] **John** answered them all, "I baptize you with water, but one who is more powerful than I am is coming. I am not worthy to untie the strap of his sandals. He will baptize you with the Holy Spirit and fire. [17] His winnowing shovel is in his hand to clear his threshing floor and gather the wheat into his barn, but the chaff he will burn with fire that never goes out." [18] Then, along with many other exhortations, he proclaimed good news to the people.

■ A GOOD QUESTION [V. 10]

When reading the Gospels, it's always helpful to examine the responses of an audience. The question the crowds asked John, "What then should we do?" (v. 10), is a good one. They wanted to know what repentance should look like. John responded by calling the crowds to meet material needs. He answered the general population: be compassionate—give away your excess food and clothing; the tax collectors: work justly; and the soldiers: be content.

■ CHARACTER STUDY

JOHN THE BAPTIST [V. 16]

John the Baptist is a central figure in the Gospels. His birth narrative precedes that of Jesus (see Luke 1). The son of Elizabeth (Mary's cousin) and Zechariah, John was the forerunner of Jesus' ministry. Jesus said John was greater than all of the Old Testament prophets (Luke 7:28).

John's ministry was prophesied in Malachi 3:1: "See, I am going to send my messenger, and he will clear the way before me. Then the Lord you seek will suddenly come to his temple, the Messenger of the covenant you delight in—see, he is coming," says the LORD of Armies." In this verse we see that John's preaching would be a message of repentance that would make the way straight for people before the coming of the Messiah.

EXAMINE

Gain a deeper appreciation for what the biblical text says.

Read the following passage from Isaiah and respond to the questions that follow.

ISAIAH 40:3-5

³ A voice of one crying out:
Prepare the way of the LORD in the wilderness;
make a straight highway for our God in the desert.
⁴ Every valley will be lifted up,
and every mountain and hill will be leveled;
the uneven ground will become smooth
and the rough places, a plain.
⁵ And the glory of the LORD will appear,
and all humanity together will see it,
for the mouth of the LORD has spoken.

Why did John quote these words? What was he trying to get his audience to understand?

Where do we see God's grace in this passage?

APPLY

Recognize that the Bible calls us to obedience and to respond to God with our lives.

Billions of people around the world don't have anyone sharing a message of salvation with them. What are we to do about this tragedy? How can we pray, give, and go to see God's glory and name known among the nations?

What could happen if we repented of our materialism and leveraged our possessions so that a world in need could see the salvation of our God?

Have you ever come to the point of repenting of your sin and confessing your need for the transforming power of the gospel?

PRAY

Respond to God with praise, thanksgiving, confession, and obedience.

Record a prayer to God in light of today's reading.

02

Physical
Need

START

Welcome to session 2 of **Something Needs to Change.** *Use these questions to begin the conversation.*

> How did God work in your heart as you thought about biblical repentance? What captured your attention from last week's personal study?

This week we'll talk about urgent physical need. We'll hear gut-wrenching stories of desperate need in mountain villages. Together we'll think about a gospel response to urgent physical need at home and around the world.

> Share a time when you were struck by an urgent physical need in the world around you.

Ask someone to pray. Then watch the video, "Day 2: Physical Need." Encourage group members to follow along, using the participant guide on pages 175–76 or at LifeWay.com/SomethingNeedstoChange.

To access video sessions, subscribe to SmallGroup.com or visit LifeWay.com/SomethingNeedstoChange.

DISCUSS

Use these questions to discuss the video teaching in your group.

One purpose of this study is to take you on a journey to see the beauty and the brokenness of the Himalayas. Today David shared some particularly difficult stories: a man losing his eye to infection, people dying of preventable disease, and traffickers taking advantage of vulnerable families. When confronted with such desperate need, we aren't always sure how to respond.

> **What stirs in your soul when you hear stories of urgent physical need?**

> **What's your typical response to physical suffering? To be momentarily appalled and move on? To do something? Why does a compassionate response involve both a visceral reaction and a desire to take action?**

David confessed that his typical response to urgent physical need is to walk away. Perhaps your response is similar. Maybe you simply don't know what to do or how to engage. Whatever the reason, Christians shouldn't walk away from need. On the contrary, Jesus calls us to run to need.

Refer to Luke 4:16-21 for the following questions.

> **Based on these verses, what kind of people did Jesus seek to serve? Why should we pay attention to the kind of people Jesus served?**

> **David stated that needs he saw in the mountains evoked a lot of *why* questions. When have you seen suffering that led you to ask God, "Why?"**

When confronted with physical suffering, it is natural to ask God *why*. However, why questions should always lead to *what* questions. Jesus wasn't content to look at suffering and move on. He took action.

Refer to Luke 5:12-15 for the following questions.

What did Jesus do when He encountered urgent physical need? Why should our *why* questions ultimately lead to *what* questions?

What made Jesus' response to the man with leprosy so countercultural? How does your response to physical need compare with Jesus' response?

In Luke 5 Jesus touched a man whom society deemed untouchable and unclean. Jesus didn't turn from need; He ran to need. The Gospels are filled with accounts when Jesus alleviated suffering, healed sickness, and treated people with mercy.

However, if we're not careful, it's dangerously possible to live our Christian lives insulated and isolated from urgent need around us. A Christian's impulse should be to run to need and proclaim the goodness, grace, and favor of our God to those in need.

What urgent physical needs exist in our community? List as many as you can think of. What can we do as a group to begin meeting those needs?

PRAYER

Father, please help us see the needs around us as You do. Help us care as You care. When we were blind, oppressed captives, You came and set us free. Looking into Your Word, we see an example and a call to meet urgent physical needs around us. Grant us grace to be faithful.

As you close, remind the group to complete the three personal studies that follow. Encourage them to spend time thinking about the suggestions for getting involved, located on the back of the participant guide.

The news about him spread even more, and large crowds would come together to hear him and to BE HEALED of their sicknesses.

LUKE 5:15

REFLECTIONS

Blindness

Aaron pulls us all together and says, "We're at close to five thousand feet in altitude right now, but we're about to ascend to about thirteen thousand feet. So I'd highly suggest you take this altitude medicine before we take off."

After landing, we begin our trek, captured by the majestic beauty of the mountains. "Put on your sunglasses," Aaron says as we shoulder our packs outside the teahouse. He points to the blue sky and the blazing sun. "The way the sun is shining on the snow up here, without sunglasses you'll go blind before too long. It's called snow blindness, sort of like sunburn in your eyes. And just like sunburn, by the time you notice the symptoms, it's too late. You can get blind spots or go completely blind for a day or two ... or longer."

With the others I slip the shades over my eyes as we start walking down the trail. I use the word *trail* loosely because it's more like we're trudging through the snow. But it's magnificent. We're surrounded on all sides by snow-covered peaks.

The mountain on our right is about twenty-seven thousand feet tall. To provide some perspective, we're hiking at around thirteen thousand feet, which is slightly lower than the height of Pikes Peak in Colorado. So right next to us we're looking at a mountain that's like Pikes Peak stacked on top of another Pikes Peak!

After hiking up and down several small rises, in about five hundred yards we come to a village with only a few homes. As we enter the village, a man steps out of his house. He's wearing a tattered beige shirt and a torn brown jacket with holes that no doubt prevent it from fulfilling its purpose. His jet-black hair, gray beard, and rough bronze skin look as if they haven't been washed for weeks. But none of these attributes are what stick out about this man; I notice that he's missing an eye.

Aaron greets him in the local language, and the man, extremely soft-spoken, quietly responds, looking down with his one eye.

"What's your name?" Aaron asks in English as he motions for Nabin to translate. Though Aaron knows much of the local language, Nabin is originally from these villages and is also proficient in English, so he serves as a translator.

The man looks up, and as I look into his eyes, I can see into his skull. "Kamal," he responds, covering the hole in his face with a cottonlike swab.

After a few minutes of small talk, Aaron says to Kamal, "May I ask what happened to your eye?"

Again looking down, Kamal answers, "A couple of months ago it became infected. At first it itched and watered. I didn't think much about it, but then it got worse. I felt a sharp pain in my head. It didn't stop for many days. Finally, my eye fell out."

Aaron asks more questions, and Kamal shares that his cheek is caving in and even his hearing is failing. As we listen, we realize what's happening. With no medicine in these mountains available to Kamal, he has an infection that's quickly overtaking his entire head and may even end his life.

Aaron shifts the conversation in a more spiritual direction and asks, "Have you ever heard of Jesus?"

Kamal looks back, confused. "No, who's that?"

It sure seems as though Kamal has never even heard that name. His response seems like he's being asked about a man he's never met who lives in a nearby village. Aaron begins to tell the story of Jesus, but Kamal seems confused about a man who lived two thousand years ago. When Aaron finishes, Kamal just looks down and quietly says, "I need help for my eye."

Aaron has helped start a clinic farther down the mountain, and he tells Kamal he will work to get him some help. "May I pray for you?" Aaron asks Kamal.

Though still obviously confused, Kamal answers, "Yes."

Standing up to our knees in the snow, shivering from the cold, we gather around Kamal and pray for God to help him in the name of Jesus.

PERSONAL STUDY 1

Slowly and intentionally read the Scriptures.

READ LUKE 4:16-30.

LUKE 4:16-21

[16] He came to Nazareth, where he had been brought up. As usual, he entered the synagogue on the Sabbath day and stood up to read. [17] The scroll of the prophet Isaiah was given to him, and unrolling the scroll, he found the place where it was written:

[18] **The Spirit of the Lord is on me,**
because he has anointed me
to preach good news to the poor.
He has sent me
to proclaim release to the captives
and recovery of sight to the blind,
to set free the oppressed,
[19] **to proclaim the year of the Lord's favor.**

[20] He then rolled up the scroll, gave it back to the attendant, and sat down. And the eyes of everyone in the synagogue were fixed on him. [21] He began by saying to them, "Today as you listen, this Scripture has been fulfilled."

■ CROSS-REFERENCE

WHY ISAIAH 61:1-2?

This passage answers the question of why Jesus came. Of all the places in Isaiah He could have read from, Jesus chose this specific passage to announce the reason He came. Quoting Isaiah 61:1-2, Jesus gave a mission statement for His ministry and revealed what kind of Messiah He would be. As we saw in Luke 2 with the announcement to the shepherds, Luke 4 zeroes in on Jesus' ministry to the poor and lowly.

THE SPIRIT OF THE LORD [V. 18]

The one true God had broken into history to save His people from their sins. A Savior had been born. Jesus alone can save people from their sins. Luke intended the reader to see the meaning of Jesus' words in terms of rescue or delivery from peril, in both its physical and spiritual senses.

GOOD NEWS

Although these verses refer to a spiritual state and can thus apply to materially rich or poor people, Jesus clearly focused His earthly ministry on the vulnerable and marginalized in society. As Jesus would later say, the sick need a doctor; the healthy don't (see Luke 5:31). Often people who are physically needy are more inclined to realize their deep spiritual needs and to receive the deliverance Jesus offers.

LUKE 4:22-30

22 They were all speaking well of him and were amazed by the gracious words that came from his mouth; yet they said, "Isn't this Joseph's son?"
23 Then he said to them, "No doubt you will quote this proverb to me: 'Doctor, heal yourself. What we've heard that took place in Capernaum, do here in your hometown also.'"
24 He also said, "Truly I tell you, no prophet is accepted in his hometown. 25 But I say to you, there were certainly many widows in Israel in Elijah's days, when the sky was shut up for three years and six months while a great famine came over all the land. 26 Yet Elijah was not sent to any of them except a widow at Zarephath in Sidon. 27 And in the prophet Elisha's time, there were many in Israel who had leprosy, and yet not one of them was cleansed except Naaman the Syrian."
28 When they heard this, everyone in the synagogue was enraged. 29 They got up, drove him out of town, and brought him to the edge of the hill that their town was built on, intending to hurl him over the cliff. 30 But he passed right through the crowd and went on his way.

■ CONTEXT

ELIJAH AND ELISHA [VV. 26-27]

Jesus' response to the Nazarenes in verse 23 indicates that they were more motivated by curiosity in the healings and miracles than by real spiritual interest. Jesus used the examples of Elijah and Elisha to illustrate that prophets are never truly welcome in their hometowns. Having been rejected by their people (Israel), both men began to minister to Gentiles, Elijah to the widow in Zarephath and Elisha to Naaman the Syrian.

HOW DID THE PEOPLE RESPOND? [V. 28]

Notice the stages of response to Jesus. At first the crowds in Nazareth were amazed at Jesus' words. They couldn't believe the authority that came from this man who grew up among them. However, their amazement quickly shifted to anger as they became "enraged" (v. 28) and sought to hurl Jesus off a cliff. As we seek to meet needs and minister in Jesus' name, we must not be alarmed when people respond to us as they responded to Him.

EXAMINE

Gain a deeper appreciation for what the biblical text says.

Reread Luke 4:18-19. Notice again the types of people to whom Jesus came to minister. Each of these descriptors has a physical and a spiritual dimension. What does it mean to be physically poor, blind, held captive, and oppressed?

	PHYSICALLY	SPIRITUALLY
POOR		
BLIND		
CAPTIVE		
OPPRESSED		

How are physical and spiritual needs often connected?

APPLY

Recognize that the Bible calls us to obey God and to respond to Him with our lives.

Serving people with urgent physical needs may take us to people and places that make us uncomfortable. If you're being honest, who are the people and what are the places you would seek to avoid while meeting needs?

Where are the poor, captive, blind, and oppressed in your city? What could you do to seek and minister to the same people Jesus sought right where you are?

PRAY

Respond to God with praise, thanksgiving, confession, and obedience.

Record a prayer to God in light of today's reading.

PERSONAL STUDY 2

READ

Slowly and intentionally read the Scriptures.

READ LUKE 4:31-37.

Luke 4 brings together the why and the what of Jesus' ministry. Yesterday's passage showed us why Jesus came: to proclaim freedom and deliverance to the poor, captive, blind, and oppressed. But as David said in this week's teaching, whys always lead to whats. Armed with the knowledge of why Jesus came, over the next two days we're going to see what His ministry entailed.

LUKE 4:31-34

31 Then he went down to Capernaum, a town in Galilee, and was teaching them on the Sabbath. 32 They were astonished at his teaching because his message had **authority**. 33 In the synagogue there was a man with an unclean demonic spirit who cried out with a loud voice, 34 "Leave us alone! What do you have to do with us, Jesus of Nazareth? Have you come to destroy us? I know who you are—the Holy One of God!"

■ WORD STUDY

AUTHORITY [V. 32]

The word the Bible uses for *authority* means "to exercise control or exert a right." It pictures someone who has power at his disposal. Both in His teaching and His actions Jesus demonstrated that He has total authority.

TRUE AUTHORITY [V. 32]

As in the previous verses, Jesus was teaching with authority that astonished the people. However, teaching is only one way Jesus demonstrated His authority. His teaching was also accompanied by action. Jesus exercised His authority by casting a demon out of a man.

THE WHY BEHIND THE WHAT

We've seen that our whys must always be followed by whats, but we also need to remember the why behind the what. Jesus didn't meet this need for the sake of meeting the need. Healings and miracles in the Bible were always meant to demonstrate Jesus' unique power and to point to His identity as the Son of God. The demon recognized Jesus for who He was, just as we should when we read accounts of healings and miracles. The healing pointed back to the reason Jesus came.

LUKE 4:35-37

³⁵ But Jesus rebuked him and said, "Be silent and come out of him!" And throwing him down before them, the demon came out of him without hurting him at all.
³⁶ Amazement came over them all, and they were saying to one another, **"What is this message?** For he commands the unclean spirits with authority and power, and they come out!" ³⁷ And news about him began to go out to every place in the vicinity.

■ GOSPEL ADVANCE [VV. 36-37]

Word immediately got out that Jesus had the power to heal the oppressed. Imagine what would happen if Christians became known for their care for the oppressed in their communities. Perhaps the news of Jesus would spread the way it did in first-century Capernaum. What would change if we met needs in Jesus' name?

■ MINISTRY LIKE JESUS

When Jesus coupled proclaiming the gospel with meeting a physical need, the results were obvious. People saw a whole gospel for the whole person, as indicated by their question, "What is this message?" Healing a person oppressed by a demon opened the door for people to see Jesus' identity more clearly. When we devote our time and resources to meet urgent physical need in Jesus' name, we bear witness to our Savior.

EXAMINE

Gain a deeper appreciation for what the biblical text says.

The verses we studied today directly followed yesterday's verses (see Luke 4:16-30). Why do you think Luke organized His Gospel this way? What was he trying to show us?

How does this passage unite Jesus' concern for physical need and His concern for spiritual need?

What about Jesus' power and authority challenges you? What about Jesus' power and authority encourages you?

APPLY

Recognize that the Bible calls us to obey God and to respond to Him with our lives.

Although you may not meet someone who's possessed by a demon, you're likely around oppressed or vulnerable people every week. Where are you likely to encounter such people?

What could you do to minister to those oppressed people in Jesus' name?

What changes in our lives when we meet physical need for the purpose of meeting deeper spiritual need?

PRAY

Respond to God with praise, thanksgiving, confession, and obedience.

Record a prayer to God in light of today's reading.

PERSONAL STUDY 3

READ

Slowly and intentionally read the Scriptures.

READ LUKE 4:38-44.

Today we continue to see Jesus minister to the sick and afflicted. Jesus didn't give mere lip service to His purpose; He lived it out.

CONTEXT

In the first century, a high fever was a serious illness. Luke, the doctor, used an ancient medical term to describe the illness afflicting Peter's mother-in-law. Without modern medicine this disease could be fatal. It was clear to those around the ill woman that Jesus would be able to help her.

LUKE 4:38-41

³⁸ After he left the synagogue, he entered Simon's house. Simon's mother-in-law was suffering from a high fever, and they asked him about her. ³⁹ So he stood over her and rebuked the fever, and it left her. She got up immediately and began to serve them. ⁴⁰ When the sun was setting, all those who had anyone sick with various diseases brought them to him. As he laid his hands on each one of them, he healed them. ⁴¹ Also, demons were coming out of many, shouting and saying, "You are the Son of God!" But he rebuked them and would not allow them to speak, because they knew he was the Christ.

REBUKED TO SERVE [V. 39]

Jesus instantly healed the devastating disease. As soon as Jesus rebuked the sickness, the woman got up and began to serve them. Though we may not witness such a miracle, we can bring relief to people who are suffering. People all over the world are dying of preventable diseases like the fever we read about here. Christians have a duty and a responsibility to meet these needs with the compassion of Jesus.

PERSONAL HEALINGS [V. 40]

Throngs of people flocked to Jesus to be healed of their sicknesses and diseases. Luke, once again emphasizing Jesus' ministry to the lowly, showed Jesus' personal care for each sick person. They weren't numbers or quotas but people made in the image of God, who needed to be healed. Jesus could have healed each of them with a word, but He touched them and demonstrated that each one was valuable to Him.

BE WITH THE FATHER [V. 42]

Jesus went to a deserted place to pray because all He did flowed from His relationship with His Father. Meeting needs and serving others can become just another religious activity if we don't make time to stop and replenish our fellowship with the Father. To maintain the purpose and focus behind our ministry, we must continually return to God's Word and to prayer. Strengthening our connection with Jesus ensures that His life is evident in our lives as we meet physical need.

LUKE 4:42-44

42 When it was day, he went out and made his way to **a deserted place**. But the crowds were searching for him. They came to him and tried to keep him from leaving them. 43 But he said to them, "It is necessary for me to **proclaim the good news** about the kingdom of God to the **other towns** also, because I was sent for this purpose." 44 And he was preaching in the synagogues of Judea.

GOSPEL PURPOSE [v. 43]

Eventually Jesus left Capernaum, but don't miss the reason He left: other cities needed His message. Jesus never lost His focus on the bigger picture. Everywhere He went, people came to Him to be healed and helped, but eventually He had to move on. Why? Because His purpose to preach the good news to the poor, captive, blind, and oppressed required Him to move on to the next town and region. Whether we're called to go around the world or to stay in one place, our calling to take the gospel to those who have never heard remains the same.

EXAMINE

Gain a deeper appreciation for what the biblical text says.

Reread Luke 4:38. How does urgency often drive people to Jesus?

LUKE 4:38

³⁸ After he left the synagogue, he entered Simon's house. Simon's mother-in-law was suffering from a high fever, and they asked him about her.

Meeting physical needs can be exhausting. It required a lot of Jesus, and it will require a lot of us. Why is it important to find "a deserted place" (v. 42) to spend time alone with our Father?

What drove Jesus to move on and continue ministering in other places? What does that pattern teach us about our motivation in ministry?

APPLY

Recognize that the Bible calls us to obey God and to respond to Him with our lives.

Jesus was absolutely committed to proclaiming the kingdom and to demonstrating the kingdom through service. Why is it easier for many of us to talk about meeting needs than to actually meet needs?

What are we missing about Jesus if the way we live never changes?

People sought Jesus as He was trying to spend time alone with His Father. How should we respond when the opportunity to meet a need interrupts our schedule?

PRAY

Respond to God with praise, thanksgiving, confession, and obedience.

Record a prayer to God in light of today's reading.

03

Spiritual Need

START

Welcome to session 3 of Something Needs to Change. *Use these questions to begin the conversation.*

As you considered urgent physical needs last week, what ways did you identify to meet those needs right where you are?

Last week we examined our calling to meet urgent physical need. This week we'll shift our focus to urgent spiritual need. Billions of people around the globe have little or no access to the gospel. Many live and die without ever hearing the name of Jesus. How should followers of Jesus respond? That's the question we'll consider today.

Share a time when you came face-to-face with urgent spiritual need.

Ask someone to pray. Then watch the video, "Day 3: Spiritual Need." Encourage group members to follow along, using the participant guide on pages 177–78 or at LifeWay.com/SomethingNeedstoChange.

To access video sessions, subscribe to SmallGroup.com or visit LifeWay.com/SomethingNeedstoChange.

DISCUSS

Use these questions to discuss the video teaching in your group.

Do you think spiritual need is more important than physical need? Why or why not?

Less than 1 percent of the people who live in the Himalayas have ever heard the name of Jesus. Our efforts must go beyond offering material assistance if we're seeking to reach someone's deepest need. Luke's Gospel shows us the priority of spiritual need.

Refer to Luke 5:17-26 for the following questions.

What evident physical needs did the paralyzed man have? What spiritual needs did he have? What drove his friends to go to such lengths to bring their friend to Jesus?

What did Jesus recognize about this man's needs that his friends missed?

When the men dismantled the roof to bring their friend to Jesus, they believed in Jesus' power to heal. However, Jesus rightly understood that more than the ability to walk, this man needed to be reconciled to God. From this encounter with Jesus, we learn that although physical need is evident all around us, spiritual need is ultimate.

Once we understand that our deepest need is to be reconciled to God, how should that realization shape the way we minister in places like the Himalayas, where desperate physical need exists among people who have never even heard of Jesus?

How do you respond to the reality that many people in the world have never heard the name of Jesus?

For thousands of years, the spectacular beauty of the Himalayas has declared the glory of God, but the majestic peaks have never said one word about Jesus. The villagers there have never heard the most beautiful news in the world: Jesus died to save them from their sins.

Has anyone in the group been to a place where few people have heard of Jesus? If so, share your experience. What was it like? How did it open your heart to needs around you?

Going to places where the gospel isn't known brings us face-to-face with the spiritual condition of billions of people around the world. The Christian church shouldn't tolerate the fact that two thousand years after Jesus walked on earth, there are people who've never heard His name. We have the greatest news for their greatest need, and we're called to give our lives to take the gospel to them.

Who are the people in your life who need to hear the news that Jesus can save them from their sin? Record those names and close your time together praying for them.

PRAYER

Father, we pray for these people who have yet to believe in Your power to save. God, would You save them? Would You give us the opportunity to speak Your truth to them in the power of Your Spirit? We pray that in hearing the good news, they'll believe in the name of Your Son for the forgiveness of sin and be made new. We ask this in Jesus' name.

As you close, remind the group to complete the three personal studies that follow. Encourage them to spend time thinking about the suggestions for getting involved, located on the back of the participant guide.

Seeing their faith he said,
"FRIEND,
YOUR SINS ARE
FORGIVEN."

LUKE 5:20

REFLECTIONS

Sky Burial

As we keep trekking, we walk for a while on a level plateau that eventually leads us near a large pile of rocks about twenty yards off the trail. We stop, then walk over to them. The rocks are stacked in a circular mound that forms a sort of stage about as wide as a human body and as tall as I can reach with my hands. Thin wooden poles surround the rocks, and attached to the poles are white tattered flags that are blowing in the wind as we approach. The site seems to have hosted some sort of ceremony. Aaron gathers us to explain what has gone on here.

"What's called a sky burial took place here. In Buddhist belief, once a person dies, their spirit is reincarnated in the body of another person, animal, or object. Such reincarnation occurs in endless cycles of life and suffering until a spirit potentially reaches a state of nirvana. Consequently, when someone dies, their corpse no longer has any value. It's merely a shell meant to be discarded by those who remain."

Aaron pauses and moves a bit closer to the mound of rocks.

"Instead of burying the body in the mountains," he continues, "which is hard to do in rugged terrain, Buddhist monks bring the body out to a burial site like this early in the morning. Family members and friends also come, though they stay at a distance. The monks involved in the ceremony are called body breakers.

"Not everybody does this, and it happens less often now than it happened a hundred years ago. But as is evidenced by this burial site, this happened not long ago right here."

"How does it work?" asks Chris.

"Together the monks use ritual knives to saw off limbs and slice the body into pieces," Aaron answers. "As each piece is cut, it's placed on top of the rock mound, where vultures then descend and eat. After the flesh and organs have been consumed by the birds, the body breakers use mallets to crush the bones. The purpose of the ceremony is to discard every part of the body so that none of it is left."

Honestly, this is hard information to digest. What he's describing sounds like something that might happen in a meat-processing plant back home. Without Aaron's explanation we could walk by this pile of rocks and the fluttering flags and have no idea about the pagan rituals performed here.

Aaron definitely has our attention: "These physical actions are loaded with spiritual meaning for Buddhists living in these mountain valleys. Some believe a sky burial is a visible picture of a person's soul being offered to the spirits or gods in the mountains as that soul moves on to a new incarnation. Many believe it's a sign of compassion for creation to use a corpse to feed birds and provide nutrients to nature. All believe it's a picture of the emptiness of the body alongside an endless cycle of suffering for the soul."

As I listen and look at the site of this sky burial, my mind starts to shift toward what seems like a completely different focus than I had yesterday. A day ago, in village after village, I was confronted in these mountains with urgent physical need. But the focus at the start of this day isn't on physical need, as important as that is, but instead on spiritual need. It's overwhelming to stand in a place where just a few days before, a man, woman, or child's body was being carved, crushed, and offered to the birds. It's even more overwhelming to think about where that man, woman, or child's spirit is now.

As important as that body's physical needs were, we're now getting an unforgettable reminder that a time comes when the body exists no more. And what happens after that point in time really matters. It matters for that man, woman, or child. It matters for every person in these mountains.

And it doesn't just matter now.

It matters forever.

Spend a few minutes praying for people around the world who've believed the lie of Buddhism. Ask that God will open their eyes to His glory and will send witnesses to tell them of His grace.

PERSONAL STUDY 1

READ

Slowly and intentionally read the Scriptures.

READ LUKE 7:11-17.

Several accounts in the Gospel of Luke depict Jesus' power and ability to save. We'll look at a few of them in this week's personal studies.

At this point in His ministry, Jesus was very popular. Crowds followed Him everywhere He went. Although some of these followers were genuine, many of them were staying around only because they wanted to see Jesus perform miracles. However, Jesus performed all of His miracles to demonstrate His unique authority as the Son of God.

■ GEOGRAPHY

NAIN [V. 11]
A village southeast of Nazareth

LUKE 7:11-13

¹¹ Afterward he was on his way to a town called Nain. His disciples and a **large crowd** were traveling with him. ¹² Just as he neared the gate of the town, a dead man was being carried out. He was his mother's only son, and she was a **widow**. A large crowd from the city was also with her. ¹³ When the **Lord** saw her, he had compassion on her and said, "Don't weep."

TITLES OF JESUS

THE LORD [V. 13]
Although the angels announced in Luke 2:11 that Jesus was the Lord, this is the first time Luke narratively referred to Jesus as Lord. He did this to emphasize Jesus' authority in the event that would happen next. Only God is sovereign over life. Seeing the funeral procession, Jesus was moved with compassion to act on the widow's behalf.

■ CONTEXT

WIDOW [V. 12]
The town of Nain was small, and the city seemed to be sharing the widow's grief with her, which was compounded by her dire circumstances. In the first century, there was no safety net for vulnerable women beyond their families. The fact that this woman lost her husband as well as her only son put her in a perilous economic situation. She now had no one to provide for her.

LARGE CROWDS

We've seen that crowds followed Jesus everywhere, but here we also see that these crowds had an incomplete view of who Jesus was. They believed He was merely a great prophet. After all, Elijah had also raised someone from the dead. As in Elijah's case, they believed Jesus was merely another man through whom God's power was mediated. They didn't understand that, as the Son of God, Jesus Himself possessed the power of God. Nevertheless, they spread the news about what they had seen and heard throughout the surrounding area.

LUKE 7:14-17

¹⁴ Then he came up and **touched the open coffin**, and the pall-bearers stopped. And he said, "Young man, I tell you, get up!" ¹⁵ The dead man sat up and began to speak, and Jesus gave him to his mother. ¹⁶ Then fear came over everyone, and they glorified God, saying, "A great prophet has risen among us," and "God has visited his people." ¹⁷ This report about him went throughout Judea and all the vicinity.

■ HISTORICAL CONTEXT

FUNERALS [V. 14]

Traditional Jewish funerals included an open coffin. When Jesus reached out to touch it, people would have undoubtedly been shocked because touching a dead body would have made Him cere-monially unclean. Yet that isn't what happened here. At a word from Jesus, the formerly deceased person began to live again.

EXAMINE

Gain a deeper appreciation for what the biblical text says.

What does Luke 7:11-17 teach us about Jesus' unique power and authority?

What does Jesus' care for the widow teach us about His heart for us?

Why is it important that we believe Jesus is both willing and able to raise the dead as the Bible tells us?

Why do you think the crowds didn't recognize Jesus' identity?

APPLY

Recognize that the Bible calls us to obey God and to respond to Him with our lives.

If we truly believe Jesus is sovereign over life and death, what changes about the way we live? How is this belief changing your life?

How can we model Jesus' individual and specific care for people who have not entered into a relationship with Jesus? How could our acts of compassion introduce opportunities to tell about God's grace?

PRAY

Respond to God with praise, thanksgiving, confession, and obedience.

Record a prayer to God in light of today's reading.

PERSONAL STUDY 2

READ

Slowly and intentionally read the Scriptures.

READ LUKE 7:36-50.

LUKE 7:36-39

³⁶ Then one of the **Pharisees** invited him to eat with him. He entered the Pharisee's house and reclined at the table. ³⁷ And **a woman in the town who was a sinner** found out that Jesus was reclining at the table in the Pharisee's house. She brought an alabaster jar of perfume ³⁸ and stood behind him at his feet, weeping, and began to wash his feet with her tears. She wiped his feet with her hair, kissing them and anointing them with the perfume.

³⁹ When the Pharisee who had invited him saw this, he said to himself, "This man, if he were a prophet, would know who and what kind of woman this is who is touching him — she's a sinner!"

■ HISTORICAL CONTEXT

PHARISEES [V. 36]

The Pharisees were a religious group characterized by strict adherence to the Old Testament commandments, a great concern for ritual purity, and close observance of the traditions of the elders. They frequently initiated disputes with Jesus.

AN EXPENSIVE OFFERING [V. 37]

Alabaster, a type of stone, likely indicates that the perfume contained inside the jar was expensive. Therefore, the offering the woman offered Jesus was of great value.

■ LOOKING DEEPER

A SINFUL WOMAN [V. 37]

The woman described as a sinner in verse 37 was likely a prostitute. The actions she took would have been seen as inappropriate and highly controversial by most observers, as illustrated by the Pharisee's response.

However, the woman's willingness to violate social taboos and give such a costly offering to Jesus while throwing herself at His feet demonstrates that she knew something the Pharisee didn't. She was a sinner who needed God's forgiveness, and she believed Jesus was able to absolve her of her sin and shame. She saw something in Jesus that the Pharisee missed.

Notice that the woman's faith in Jesus, not her actions, resulted in the forgiveness of her sins. Her actions only outwardly demonstrated a heart that had been changed by God.

LUKE 7:40-50

[40] Jesus replied to him, "Simon, **I have something to say to you**." He said, "Say it, teacher."

[41] "A creditor had two debtors. One owed five hundred denarii, and the other fifty. [42] Since they could not pay it back, he graciously forgave them both. So, which of them will love him more?"

[43] Simon answered, "I suppose the one he forgave more."

"You have judged correctly," he told him. [44] Turning to the woman, he said to Simon, "Do you see this woman? I entered your house; you gave me no water for my feet, but she, with her tears, has washed my feet and wiped them with her hair. [45] You gave me no kiss, but she hasn't stopped kissing my feet since I came in. [46] You didn't anoint my head with olive oil, but she has anointed my feet with perfume. [47] Therefore I tell you, her many sins have been forgiven; that's why she loved much. But the one who is forgiven little, loves little." [48] Then he said to her, "Your sins are forgiven."

[49] Those who were at the table with him began to say among themselves, "Who is this man who even forgives sins?"

[50] And he said to the woman, "Your faith has saved you. Go in peace."

■ LITERARY CONTEXT

PARABLES [VV. 40-43]

Parables are stories used to illustrate a point. Jesus often employed this teaching technique to reveal His will. The parable Jesus told is a relatively straightforward one meant to highlight the gratitude that comes from knowing our sins are forgiven.

WHAT THE SINNER SAW, THE PHARISEE MISSED [VV. 44-48]

Simon the Pharisee was an ungracious host who ignored even basic hospitality standards in His treatment of Jesus. The woman, in contrast, lavished care on Jesus. She understood that she was a sinner, while Simon didn't recognize that he was. Her actions reflected a heart that had been transformed by grace.

EXAMINE

Gain a deeper appreciation for what the biblical text says.

What did it cost this woman materially and socially to go to Jesus? How has following Jesus cost you?

If we expect to take the gospel to people who desperately need it, what should we expect it to cost us?

The Pharisees frequently missed the plain truth about Jesus. In what ways can you identify with them? When have you missed the point of Jesus' teachings?

What does your life look like when you truly understand what it means to be forgiven?

APPLY

Recognize that the Bible calls us to obey God and to respond to Him with our lives.

All sinners transformed by grace have been forgiven of a debt that was too large to repay. How do your actions reveal your inner faith in Christ? Do you live as someone who has received much grace?

We live in a world where many people haven't heard the name of Jesus. Why should the grace we've received from Jesus motivate us to tell anyone who will listen about that grace?

The sinful woman lived with an urgency and a desperate need to know Jesus. How does your desire to know Jesus and make Him known compare with hers?

PRAY

Respond to God with praise, thanksgiving, confession, and obedience.

Record a prayer to God in light of today's reading.

PERSONAL STUDY 3

READ

Slowly and intentionally read the Scriptures.

READ LUKE 8:40-56.

Today we'll look at other encounters in Jesus' ministry that reveal His authority over life and death and His ability to forgive sins.

LUKE 8:40-47

⁴⁰ When Jesus returned, the crowd welcomed him, for they were all expecting him. ⁴¹ Just then, a man named Jairus came. He was a leader of the synagogue. He fell down at Jesus's feet and pleaded with him to come to his house, ⁴² because he had an only daughter about twelve years old, and she was dying.

While he was going, the crowds were nearly crushing him. ⁴³ A woman suffering from bleeding for twelve years, who had spent all she had on doctors and yet could not be healed by any, ⁴⁴ approached from behind and touched the end of his robe. Instantly her bleeding stopped.

⁴⁵ "Who touched me?" Jesus asked.

When they all denied it, Peter said, "Master, the crowds are hemming you in and pressing against you."

⁴⁶ "Someone did touch me," said Jesus. "I know that power has gone out from me." ⁴⁷ When the woman saw that she was discovered, she came trembling and fell down before him. In the presence of all the people, she declared the reason she had touched him and how she was instantly healed.

■ INTENTIONAL CONTRAST

This passage presents two stories about desperate people.

Jairus was a father who was losing a twelve-year-old daughter. As we've heard, more than half of the children in the Himalayas die of preventable diseases by age eight. A certain kind of desperation comes to a parent who's trying to help a sick child. Falling down at Jesus' feet, a sign of complete submission, would have been uncommon for a man of such standing as a synagogue ruler.

The bleeding woman would have been considered ceremonially unclean. Because she had been bleeding for twelve years, she had been ceremonially unclean for that length of time. As a result, her contact with others would have been limited. She came to Jesus from behind because she realized that what she was doing was taboo. However, if she had come openly, the crowd might not have allowed her to reach Him. Her desperation drove her to Jesus.

FAITH THAT SAVES [V. 48]

Once again we see that a person's faith saved her. Reaching out to touch Jesus demonstrated the woman's faith, which, through God's grace, made her well. Notice that Jesus addressed her as daughter in verse 48. No longer was she hidden and alienated from society; she was clean and free.

LUKE 8:48-56

⁴⁸ "Daughter," he said to her, "your faith has saved you. Go in peace."

⁴⁹ While he was still speaking, someone came from the synagogue leader's house and said, "Your daughter is dead. **Don't bother the teacher anymore.**"

⁵⁰ When Jesus heard it, he answered him, "Don't be afraid. Only believe, and she will be saved." ⁵¹ After he came to the house, he let no one enter with him except Peter, John, James, and the child's father and mother. ⁵² Everyone was crying and mourning for her. But he said, "Stop crying, because she is not dead but asleep."

⁵³ They laughed at him, because they knew she was dead. ⁵⁴ So he took her by the hand and called out, **"Child, get up!"** ⁵⁵ **Her spirit returned, and she got up at once.** Then he gave orders that she be given something to eat. ⁵⁶ Her parents were astounded, but he instructed them to tell no one what had happened.

■ WORD STUDY

"CHILD, GET UP" [V. 54]

When Jesus raised this little girl from the dead, He used the same words her mother would have used to wake her up in the morning (see v. 54). These loving words show a compassionate understanding of the needs of the people Jesus ministered to.

POWER BEYOND DEATH [V. 55]

While Jesus stopped to heal the woman, Jairus's daughter died. The one who alerted Jairus to this painful reality encouraged him to come away and no longer bother Jesus.

The gathered crowd failed to recognize that Jesus had power that extended beyond the grave. Jesus alone has authority over life and death.

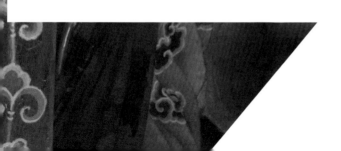

EXAMINE

Gain a deeper appreciation for what the biblical text says.

In these encounters two people with desperate physical needs approached Jesus. Why were their spiritual needs much greater than their physical needs?

Look at the response of the crowd in the house in Luke 8:53. They laughed at Jesus. How should we respond when we try to tell someone about Jesus and they believe the facts of the gospel are ridiculous or unbelievable?

How lonely and isolated must the bleeding woman have been? How lonely and isolated are people who are truly separated from God, even if they don't realize their condition? What responsibility does the church have to these people?

APPLY

Recognize that the Bible calls us to obey God and to respond to Him with our lives.

In both accounts in Luke 8 we see Jesus meeting the deep needs of people who sought Him. Whom do you know who's in a desperate situation and looking for answers?

How could you connect their need to the gospel?

What changes could you make to confront urgent spiritual need with the truth of the gospel?

PRAY

Respond to God with praise, thanksgiving, confession, and obedience.

Record a prayer to God in light of today's reading.

04

Loving God and Others

START

Welcome to session 4 of Something Needs to Change. *Use these questions to begin the conversation.*

> Last week you were asked to consider what needed to change in your life in order to respond to urgent spiritual needs around the world. How did God convict you?

Over the course of this trek through the Himalayas, we've heard some difficult stories about the urgent needs and spiritual darkness found there. You may be asking yourself, *Where do these challenges leave us? How should we respond to such needs?* The answer is surprisingly simple: live with undivided love for God and unselfish love for others.

> Describe a time when other people loved you as they loved themselves.

> What did their willingness to go out of their way to care for you mean to you?

Ask someone to pray. Then watch the video, "Day 4: Loving God and Others." Encourage group members to follow along, using the participant guide on pages 179–80 or at LifeWay.com/SomethingNeedstoChange.

To access video sessions, subscribe to SmallGroup.com or visit LifeWay.com/SomethingNeedstoChange.

DISCUSS

Use these questions to discuss the video teaching in your group.

Think about the church David described in the Himalayas. How is this church both like and unlike your church?

When you became a follower of Jesus, you entered an eternal community composed of people from every corner of the globe. Though the church we heard about in the Himalayas may be different from ours, those brothers and sisters are similar to us in their commitment to what matters most: an abiding love for God that manifests itself in committed care for people. In the parable of the good Samaritan, Jesus shows us what it looks like to love people out of reverence for God.

Refer to Luke 10:25-37 for the following questions.

What would you say is the central point of this parable?

What might this story look like if it played out in our community?

What types of people do we esteem less or avoid helping?

The parable of the good Samaritan is not chiefly about helping people in need. It's about our need for a new heart, filled with undivided love for God and unselfish love for others. That kind of heart can come only through the transforming work of God's grace.

The teacher of the law asked Jesus a question to try and justify himself. What kinds of excuses do we make to justify our disobedience to God's commands?

What should motivate our desire to help people in need? What do we often make our motivation instead?

The gospel, not guilt, motivates us to help our neighbors in need. The gospel came to us when we ourselves were needy and desperate. Once you realize that you're the one in need, you don't try to justify yourself. A heart changed by the gospel obeys not from obligation but from the fruit of God's work in our lives.

> How can you ensure that this kind of change is motivated by the gospel and not by guilt?

All of us have shown the kind of love the Samaritan showed to the injured man. The problem is, we typically show that level of care only for ourselves. The Bible teaches us that a better, more satisfying life comes when we give ourselves away for others, as Jesus did for us in the gospel.

> What might look different in your life if you loved other people as much as you love yourself?

PRAYER

Jesus, thank You for your grace that motivates us to care for others as You've cared for us. Lord, please transform us into people who are marked by undivided love for You and by unselfish, unqualified love for our neighbors. Give us eyes to see the neighbors You've placed around us and grace to have compassion on them.

As you close, remind the group to complete the three personal studies that follow. Encourage them to spend time thinking about the suggestions for getting involved, located on the back of the participant guide.

Jesus told him,

"GO AND DO THE SAME."

LUKE 10:37

REFLECTIONS

Tears into Tactics

"On the first day of this trek, in the first teahouse we visited right after we got off the helicopter, you told us that you first came up these mountains twenty years ago with your college friends. You said you were planning to hike for weeks, but at your stop that first night, you encountered something that kept you from sleeping. You said you cried all night long, and then you packed your bags and went back down the mountain."

He nods, so I ask, "What was it that you encountered? What made you head back down the mountain?"

Aaron briefly smiles. Then his expression turns serious. "I met a trafficker," he says. "My friends and I were eating dinner at a rest stop, and we were talking with a man who started bragging to us about all the girls he had met in the mountains. He told us that he would take the girls out of their impoverished conditions into the city for work. He described how the girls made a living while men like him got pleasure."

Tears swell in Aaron's eyes as he continues, his voice now trembling. "The way this man talked about these girls was maddening. He viewed them as nothing more than objects to be used and abused in whatever way he and others wanted."

"Just as soon as the man finished talking," Aaron continues, "he said he needed to go, and he got up from the table and left. As I watched him walk away, I sat there in shock. For a few moments the guys around me talked about the horrible things this man had said, but before long they were talking about how eager they were to get to bed and start hiking again the next morning."

Aaron pauses again, obviously moved as he relives the moment. "But I couldn't get my mind off what that man had said. I was totally numb. I couldn't believe what I'd just heard. And I couldn't stop thinking about it. I couldn't stop thinking about those little girls."

Tears now fall down Aaron's face as he says, "I went to bed that night and just lay there crying all night long. Then I got up the next morning, and I knew I couldn't continue go on as if nothing had happened. I told my buddies to go on without me. I hiked down the trail by myself, and for the past twenty years I've been working to turn those tears into tactics for making God's grace known in these mountains."

As we walk next to each other, I have no idea what to say in response to Aaron's story. Aaron can tell I'm wrestling with a lot, and he says, "Your question is a good one but just a little bit off. You asked me what made me head back down the mountain that morning, but the answer isn't what. The answer is who. David, God did a work in my heart that night that caused me to go back down that mountain. God created in me a love for these people and a longing to show His love to them in any way I can with my life. That's the only reason I'm here right now."

About that time the path narrows, and Aaron eventually moves in front of me. "We're about to head up a steep trail on the side of this mountain," he says. "Take your time and watch your step."

As we start the incline, the irony isn't lost on me. To a kind of love that goes beyond all my religious learning or sense of religious responsibility. A kind of love that only God can create. A kind of love that causes you to change the plans you might have had for your life or your family or your future. A kind of costly, uncomfortable love that's neither complacent nor content to protect yourself from the needs of those around you. As I start up the trail, I think, *This is the kind of love I long to mark my life.*

PERSONAL STUDY 1

READ

Slowly and intentionally read the Scriptures.

READ LUKE 10:25-37.

Although we looked at this section of Scripture during the group study, it merits a further look. This parable may be familiar to you, but try to consider it with fresh eyes today. Jesus used this story to teach essential truths about what it means to be undivided in our love for God and unselfish in our love for our neighbors.

LUKE 10:25-29

²⁵ Then an expert in the law stood up to test him, saying, "Teacher, what must I do to inherit eternal life?"

²⁶ "What is written in the law?" he asked him. "How do you read it?"

²⁷ He answered, **"Love the Lord your God with all your heart, with all your soul, with all your strength, and with all your mind,"** and **"your neighbor as yourself."**

²⁸ "**You've answered correctly**," he told him. "Do this and you will live."

²⁹ But wanting to justify himself, he asked Jesus, "And who is my neighbor?"

■ CROSS REFERENCES [V. 27]

To answer Jesus' question, the expert in the law quoted two parts of the Old Testament that summarized the whole law.

UNDIVIDED LOVE FOR GOD, DEUTERONOMY 6:4-5. These verses are known as the Shema, which is the first Hebrew word in the original verses. The Shema is a call to love the Lord with our heart (emotions); soul (the immaterial part of us); strength (will); and, as Jesus added, mind (thoughts and reason). In other words, we're to love God with all we are.

UNSELFISH LOVE FOR OTHERS, LEVITICUS 19:18. A foundational element of God's law is consideration for others. Because all people are made in the image of God, all people, without qualification, are worthy of our love and respect.

■ A GOOD ANSWER [V. 28]

Surprisingly, the lawyer correctly answered Jesus' question. The problem, as Jesus revealed, wasn't that the lawyer didn't know the law but that he didn't obey it. Likewise, none of us perfectly obey these laws. We fail to love God and others all the time. In order to live these commands, we need to have a heart that has been transformed by the gospel.

■ THE SETTING [V. 30]

The road from Jerusalem to Jericho was a steep, seventeen-mile, downhill road filled with caves, rocks, and crevasses. The landscape made this road a common place for robbers to take advantage of unsuspecting travelers.

LUKE 10:30-37

³⁰ Jesus took up the question and said: "A **man** was going down from Jerusalem to Jericho and fell into the hands of robbers. They stripped him, beat him up, and fled, leaving him half dead. ³¹ A **priest** happened to be going down that road. When he saw him, he passed by on the other side. ³² In the same way, a **Levite**, when he arrived at the place and saw him, passed by on the other side. ³³ But a **Samaritan** on his journey came up to him, and when he saw the man, he had compassion. ³⁴ He went over to him and bandaged his wounds, pouring on olive oil and wine. Then he put him on his own animal, brought him to an inn, and took care of him. ³⁵ The next day he took out two denarii, gave them to the innkeeper, and said, 'Take care of him. When I come back I'll reimburse you for whatever extra you spend.'

³⁶ "Which of these three do you think proved to be a neighbor to the man who fell into the hands of the robbers?"

³⁷ "The one who showed mercy to him," he said.

Then Jesus told him, "Go and do the same."

■ THE CHARACTERS

To understand this parable, we need to understand the characters involved. Because we're removed by time and culture from the Bible, we must dig a little deeper to discover who these people are and the way a first-century audience would have heard Jesus' words.

A MAN. The traveler on the Jericho road isn't fully described because he's not the focus of the story; the responses of the other characters are. The traveler is brutally beaten and left on the side of the road to die.

A PRIEST. A descendant of Aaron who ministered in the temple, this man would have been seen as a devout religious figure, making him the most inclined to care for the man. Instead, he was more concerned about his own safety and about remaining ritually clean to be involved with caring for a dead or mortally injured man.

A LEVITE. A Levite was a member of the tribe of Levi who assisted the priest in his duties for the temple. If the priest didn't stop, surely this Levite would. Yet he too passed by the man without offering help.

A SAMARITAN. Though the audience may have thought an Israelite would have come down the road next, Jesus added a twist by introducing a Samaritan. The Jews hated the Samaritans, believing they were half-breeds who had intermarried with foreigners. It would have been unthinkable that a Samaritan would stop to help a Jew. Yet that's exactly what happened. The Samaritan unselfishly took care of the wounded Jew at his own expense.

EXAMINE

Gain a deeper appreciation for what the biblical text says.

What stood out to you as you read this parable?

What did the lawyer's question reveal about his heart?

If this parable were retold in today's context, who would these characters be?

What did the expert in the law misunderstand about God's character and about the law itself?

APPLY

Recognize that the Bible calls us to obey God and to respond to Him with our lives.

Why does the gospel motivate us to love our neighbor as ourselves?

Who's a person in your community to whom you could tangibly show the love of God through unselfish love?

PRAY

Respond to God with praise, thanksgiving, confession, and obedience.

Record a prayer to God in light of today's reading.

PERSONAL STUDY 2

READ

Slowly and intentionally read the Scriptures.

READ LUKE 11:1-4.

Luke's Gospel is unique for the attention Luke gave to Jesus' prayer life. If we're going to become people who love God and love others well, we must become people of prayer.

LUKE 11:1-4

11 **He was praying in a certain place**, and when he finished, one of his disciples said to him, "Lord, **teach us to pray**, just as John also taught his disciples."
² He said to them, "Whenever you pray, say,
    Father,
    your name be honored as holy.
    Your kingdom come.
  ³ Give us each day our daily bread.
  ⁴ And forgive us our sins,
    for we ourselves also forgive everyone
    in debt to us.
    And do not bring us into temptation."

■ A MODEL PRAYER

The disciples saw Jesus praying and asked Him to teach them how to pray. Jesus' response has been called the Lord's Prayer or the Model Prayer. Luke's version of this prayer is similar but shorter than the more familiar version in Matthew's Gospel (see 6:9–13).

It would have been unusual for a Jewish person to refer to God as Father, but it was the primary way Jesus spoke to and about God. Through Jesus we relate to God as a loving Father whose name we desire to be known and renowned in all the earth. The prayer includes requests for God's will to be honored, our lives to align with His will, and our needs to be met.

TEACHING ON PRAYER FROM THE GOSPEL OF LUKE

REFERENCE	JESUS PRAYING
Luke 3:21	Jesus prays at His baptism.
Luke 5:15-16	Jesus prays after performing miracles.
Luke 6:12-13	Jesus prays when choosing His disciples.
Luke 9:18-22	Jesus prays before predicting His death.
Luke 9:29	Jesus prays at the transfiguration.
Luke 10:17-21	Jesus prays when the seventy disciples return.
Luke 11:1	Jesus prays before teaching the disciples to pray.
Luke 22:31-32	Jesus prays for Peter.
Luke 22:39-46	Jesus prays in Gethsemane.
Luke 23:34,46	Jesus prays on the cross.

REFERENCE	JESUS' TEACHING ON PRAYER
Luke 6:28	Pray for those who mistreat you.
Luke 11:2	How to pray
Luke 10:2	Pray for laborers in the field.
Luke 11:5-8	Persist in prayer.
Luke 18:1-8	The parable of the unrighteous judge
Luke 20:46-47	Warning against empty prayers
Luke 22:40	Pray against temptation.

EXAMINE

Gain a deeper appreciation for what the biblical text says.

Read the Lord's Prayer again and highlight each individual request.

LUKE 11:2-4

2 He said to them, "Whenever you pray, say,
  Father,
  your name be honored as holy.
  Your kingdom come.
3   Give us each day our daily bread.
4   And forgive us our sins,
  for we ourselves also forgive everyone
  in debt to us.
  And do not bring us into temptation."

What do these elements teach us about how we should personally pray?

How does this prayer reflect love for God and neighbor?

APPLY

Recognize that the Bible calls us to obey God and to respond to Him with our lives.

How does God use prayer to transform our hearts and to shape our lives?

What does prayer look like in your life? When and where do you make time to pray in an intentional, unhurried way?

What are a few prayers God has answered for you over the past year?

PRAY

Respond to God with praise, thanksgiving, confession, and obedience.

Record a prayer to God in light of today's reading.

PERSONAL STUDY 3

READ

Slowly and intentionally read the Scriptures.

READ LUKE 11:5-13.

These verses, which immediately follow the Lord's Prayer, give valuable insights into the practice of prayer in a believer's life. Jesus begin with a parable in verses 5-8 and verses 9-13 expand Jesus' teaching on prayer.

LUKE 11:5-8

⁵ He also said to them: "Suppose one of you has a friend and goes to him at midnight and says to him, 'Friend, lend me three loaves of bread, ⁶ because a friend of mine on a journey has come to me, and I don't have anything to offer him.' ⁷ Then he will answer from inside and say, 'Don't bother me! The door is already locked, and my children and I have gone to bed. I can't get up to give you anything.' ⁸ I tell you, even though he won't get up and give him anything because he is his friend, yet because of his friend's **shameless boldness**, he will get up and give him as much as he needs.

■ CONTEXT

FIRST-CENTURY HOSPITALITY

In the first century, not having food to offer a guest was a serious social misstep. This insight helps explain the aggravation felt by the man when the friend knocked on his door after dark. The man in the story had likely traveled at night to avoid the heat of the day.

■ WORD STUDY

SHAMELESS BOLDNESS [V. 8]

In the original language of the New Testament, "shameless boldness" (v. 8) is one word, meaning "a lack of sensitivity to convention," "shamelessness," or even "impudence." Jesus was painting a picture of a man who was so audacious that he was unbothered by waking up a neighbor at midnight. He knew what his friend needed and was unafraid to ask for it. Jesus is telling us that this is how we should pray.

■ CONTEXT

A COMMON ARGUMENT

In these verses Jesus used a common rhetorical argument from the lesser to the greater: if an imperfect father gives good gifts, how much more willing would a perfect Father be to give His children good things?

LUKE 11:9-13

9 "So I say to you, **ask**, and it will be given to you. **Seek**, and you will find. **Knock**, and the door will be opened to you. 10 For everyone who asks receives, and the one who seeks finds, and to the one who knocks, the door will be opened. 11 What father among you, if his son asks for a fish, will give him a snake instead of a fish? 12 Or if he asks for an egg, will give him a scorpion? 13 If you then, who are evil, know how to give good gifts to your children, **how much more will the heavenly Father give the Holy Spirit to those who ask him?**"

■ WORD STUDY

ASK, SEEK, AND KNOCK [V. 9]

In the original language of the New Testament, these verbs indicate continuous action, meaning they could be translated "keep asking, keep seeking, and keep knocking." Our work in prayer should be constant and ongoing.

We should continually approach God, asking Him to give us the grace to love Him and others with an undivided heart.

■ APPLICATION

WILL GOD GIVE US WHATEVER WE ASK? [V. 13]

Jesus wasn't saying we'll get everything we ask for. He was saying, as the previous parable illustrates, that we're free to ask our Father for what we need. He never tires of hearing our requests, and He delights to give all His children good things. Jesus is teaching us that perhaps the reason we don't have is that we don't ask our Father for our needs.

EXAMINE

Gain a deeper appreciation for what the biblical text says.

Record four key truths Luke 11:5-13 teaches you about the practice of prayer.

How do these truths complement day 2's reading from the Lord's Prayer?

In what ways could God change us if we continually came boldly to Him in prayer, asking Him to help us love Him and others?

APPLY

Recognize that the Bible calls us to obey God and to respond to Him with our lives.

What needs to change in your prayer life, based on Luke 11:5-13?

Many believers struggle in the practice of prayer. Who could hold you accountable in your prayer life?

Will you commit to pray every day for the next week for God to increase your love for Him and your love for others? When will you carve out the time to make this prayer a priority?

PRAY

Respond to God with praise, thanksgiving, confession, and obedience.

Record a prayer to God in light of today's reading.

Opportunities

START

Welcome to session 5 of Something Needs to Change. *Use these questions to begin the conversation.*

> Over the past week you were asked to consider ways you could show unselfish love to your community. What ideas came to mind?

Once we're clear that following Jesus means we're committing ourselves to love God absolutely and others unselfishly, we can turn our attention to the avenues God has given us to live out that calling.

> What do you do for a living? How did you become involved in that line of work?

> What do you enjoy doing in your free time? What friendships have you formed through these interests?

Every person has God-given skills, training, talents, abilities, and passions. We've received those gifts to use for God's glory—at home and to the ends of the earth.

Ask someone to pray. Then watch the video, "Day 5: Opportunities." Encourage group members to follow along, using the participant guide on pages 181–82 or at LifeWay.com/SomethingNeedstoChange.

To access video sessions, subscribe to SmallGroup.com or visit LifeWay.com/SomethingNeedstoChange.

DISCUSS

Use these questions to discuss the video teaching in your group.

If we believe God is sovereign and is providentially leading the world to glorify Himself, then we can't believe our talents and abilities have come to us by accident. Instead of using our careers to add to our bottom line, our reputation, or any other human pursuit, God wants each of us to make our lives count with the grace He has given to us.

Refer to Luke 12:16-21 for the following questions.

Where do you see the rich man's attitude in our culture today? Where do you see it in your life?

The life that counts is rich toward God and generous toward others. Because we're disciples of Jesus, our lives should look different from the world around us. As God gives grace, we generously pour it out on others. True life is found in radical generosity toward others.

Refer to Luke 12:32-34 for the following questions.

What did Jesus mean when He called the disciples "little flock" (v. 32)? How does this term reflect His care for them?

How do these verses contrast treasure on earth with treasure in heaven? Why do we seek treasure on earth instead of the better treasure in heaven?

The life that counts gives generously because it continually rests in the love of God. Jesus called the disciples a "little flock" because He cared for them. God is a Shepherd who protects us, a Father who delights in us, and a King who provides for us. Jesus is committed to our well-being, and in these verses He tells us that life isn't found in an accumulation of possessions but in His love for us. Once we grasp that truth, the curse of materialism will be broken in our lives, and we'll freely give our resources to advance His cause in the world.

Refer to Luke 12:42-48 for the following questions.

The point of this parable is simple: when God gives much to us, we have much to invest for His glory. We've been given gifts by God to use for God. How are we using ours? How can we make our lives count by being rich toward God and generous toward others? Let's explore some possibilities.

Reread verse 48. How are you using the greatest gift God has given you—the gospel? What's required of us in our gospel witness?

End your time together by sharing and brainstorming responses to the following questions.

David shared multiple examples of people who've leveraged their careers for the gospel through their professions. How could someone use a job like yours to leverage his or her life for Jesus?

What about your other skills and interests? How could God use your passions, abilities, talents, or hobbies for His glory?

PRAYER

God, thank You for Your grace in our lives. We pray that we'll honor You by taking what You've given us and generously giving to others. We're grateful for the ways You've blessed us. Please help us leverage all You've given us to display Your glory throughout the whole world.

As you close, remind the group to complete the three personal studies that follow. Encourage them to spend time thinking about the suggestions for getting involved, located on the back of the participant guide.

From everyone who
has been given much,
MUCH WILL
BE REQUIRED;
and from the one
who has been entrusted
with much, even more
will be expected.

LUKE 12:48

REFLECTIONS

Trout and Vegetables

Freshly encouraged and exhilarated after meeting with the church the night before, the next morning I decide four days is sufficient for one set of layers, so it's time on this trek to retire them for another. I trust the new set will last the final three days. Besides, Aaron told us last night that we'd be hiking mostly downhill today and descending to a lower elevation the rest of the way, which means higher temperatures on the trails.

Aaron says, "I want to introduce you to someone else at the teahouse up ahead." So we grab our packs and follow him back onto the trail.

When we arrive at the teahouse, we walk inside and sit at a table for a late lunch (really an early dinner, since this is where we're staying tonight). A few minutes later a thick, bearded, brawny Caucasian man, who I guess to be in his midfifties, enters.

"Ben!" Aaron shouts, smiling, before the two men shake hands and slap each other on the back.

Aaron turns and introduces each of us to Ben. After he and Aaron sit down, we listen as they briefly catch up with each other. Ben relates that his wife is doing well here in the community, and his two daughters in college back in the States are getting along great. After more conversation between them, Aaron turns and says to us, "Listen, I want you all to hear what Ben does. He and his wife moved into this village a couple of years ago and are making a big difference in a pretty unique way. "Ben," Aaron says as he turns toward him, "please don't be shy. Tell them all about you, trout poop, and the gospel."

That piques our curiosity!

"Well," Ben begins with a deep Southern drawl, "I've been involved in agricultural engineering all my life back in the South—the southern U.S., that is" (as if we thought he might originally be from South Asia!). "But then I came on a trip out here with Aaron, and I saw the need for food in these villages. The soil isn't good for growing vegetables, but that led me to start thinking about ways I could help.

"So I planned another time to come back up here, and I set up a little experiment. I put some fish in a small tank with water and engineered some PVC pipes to cycle water from the tank to a platform with plants. Then I engineered that water to recycle back into the fish tank after its exposure to the plants. It's called aquaponics."

He has our total interest. None of us thought we would encounter something like this in such a remote village.

"It starts with fish poop," Ben says with passion. "The waste from the fish gets released into the water. Their waste is rich in nitrate, which is the form of nitrogen that plants use to grow. So basically, the fish poop turns into plant food. And as the plants eat the food, they clean the water for the fish, which then recycles back around for the fish to live in. So the fish and the plants help each other grow, and you have a continual supply of food and vegetables."

"I love that. How creative!" Sigs says.

"The experiment worked well the first time, but we needed to make some changes. So I came back on a third trip, this time with my wife, and we tried to use solar power to sustain the system. We were able to get that to work, and we also learned we could use bamboo as the medium to pump the water through. The plant yield was amazing, even though we were doing this on a pretty small scale. And we could see what a difference this system could make for people in these villages."

"I can't tell you how excited I was with what happened next!" Aaron says.

"That's when my wife and I decided that God was calling us here," Ben concludes. "Since God has given me the ability to create these kinds of systems, and people here who don't have enough food could live and thrive if I just used what God has given me, then we decided coming here was a no-brainer."

What skills do you have that could be used for the gospel the way Ben is using his unique skill set?

PERSONAL STUDY 1

READ

Slowly and intentionally read the Scriptures.

READ LUKE 12:13-21.

■ CONTEXT

Jesus told the parable we're reading today in response to a question over inheritance. Because rabbis settled disputes in Jewish society, the man who came to Jesus was recognizing Him as a teacher of Israel. However, Jesus refused to be drawn into the issue.

LUKE 12:13-15

¹³ **Someone from the crowd said to him**, "Teacher, tell my brother to divide the inheritance with me."
¹⁴ "Friend," he said to him, "who appointed me a judge or arbitrator over you?" ¹⁵ He then told them, "Watch out and be on guard against all **greed**, because one's life is not in the abundance of his possessions."

JESUS' RESPONSE [V. 14]

Based on Jesus' first statement to the man, it appears that the man was motivated by greed. Notice that he didn't ask Jesus to arbitrate but to give him what he wanted. In addition, Jesus knew what was inside people (see John 2:25), so He was able to see past the man's question and directly into his motivation.

■ WORD STUDY

GREED [V. 15]

Another way to translate this word in verse 15 is *covetousness*. The original word refers to an insatiable desire to have more than a person is due.

QUESTION

WAS JESUS AGAINST WEALTH?

Jesus warned against greed, not against wealth or saving per se. The greater issue was how the man stewarded what he had been given. He hadn't considered ways he could use what he had been given for a greater purpose. The parable is meant to be a warning against the complacency that comes from comfort.

LUKE 12:16-21

[16] Then he told them a parable: "A rich man's land was very productive. [17] He thought to himself, 'What should I do, since I don't have anywhere to store my crops? [18] I will do this,' he said. 'I'll tear down my barns and build bigger ones and store all my grain and my goods there. [19] Then I'll say to myself, "You have many goods stored up for many years. Take it easy; eat, drink, and enjoy yourself."'

[20] "But God said to him, 'You **fool**! This very night your life is demanded of you. And the things you have prepared — whose will they be?'

[21] "That's how it is with the one who stores up treasure for himself and is not **rich toward God**."

FOOL [V. 20]

Ironically, the man who thought he was wise was actually a fool. Hoping to show himself as prepared, he was truly unprepared for what really mattered.

RICH TOWARD GOD [V. 21]

The life that really matters is rich toward God. Instead of using all our gifts, talents, resources, and abilities for ourselves. God calls us to use them for His kingdom. When we make deposits into that account, we reap rewards in heaven that are truly not worth comparing to what we freely gave away on earth.

EXAMINE

Gain a deeper appreciation for what the biblical text says.

What does His refusal to intervene in this dispute teach us about what truly mattered to Jesus?

What does Jesus' response reveal about the man (and about us)?

What was the man's first thought after seeing the yield of his crop?

What's the difference between earthly treasures and worldly treasures (see Matt. 6:19-21)?

APPLY

Recognize that the Bible calls us to obey God and to respond to Him with our lives.

What resources do you have at your disposal (think big picture here—job, talents, savings, interests, and hobbies)? What would it look like to hoard these for yourself? What would it look like to leverage them for the gospel?

Whom do you know who uses their resources to advance the gospel?
What could you learn from their example?

PRAY

Respond to God with praise, thanksgiving, confession, and obedience.

Record a prayer to God in light of today's reading.

PERSONAL STUDY 2

READ

Slowly and intentionally read the Scriptures.

READ LUKE 10:1-9.

Today we're going to backtrack in the Gospel of Luke to consider ideas related to using our gifts for the gospel. We'll look at the way God uses prayer to call workers into the harvest.

LUKE 10:1-2

10 After this, the Lord appointed seventy-two others, and he sent them ahead of him in pairs to every town and place where he himself was about to go. ² He told them, "The harvest is **abundant**, but the workers are **few**. Therefore, pray to the Lord of the harvest to send out workers into his harvest.

■ CONTEXT

Jesus gave these directions as He sent out seventy-two disciples in pairs to minister in places to which He would later travel. These disciples would prepare the way for Jesus in those communities. When we commit to use our gifts in an unreached area, we go in Jesus' power, proclaiming His gospel to those who so desperately need Him.

THE PROBLEM

LABORERS OR HARVEST? [V. 2]

Often we tell ourselves the lie that our attempts to share the gospel won't work because people are too resistant to the gospel. Jesus begs to differ. According to Jesus, the problem isn't with the harvest but with the lack of workers. Therefore, we need to pray earnestly for God, "the Lord of the harvest" (v. 2), to send laborers.

HOSTILE TERRITORY [V. 3]

Allowing Jesus to use our gifts may not always be easy. He realizes that we're being sent out like lambs to the slaughter. An underlying idea in these verses is that affection for Jesus can't be forced. People respond in faith, yet many people are resistant to Jesus. No matter where we go in seeking to make Jesus known, we'll come across people who reject the message. In those moments remember to rely on the Lord of the harvest.

LUKE 10:3-9

³ Now go; I'm sending you out like **lambs among wolves**. ⁴ Don't carry a money-bag, traveling bag, or sandals; don't greet anyone along the road. ⁵ Whatever house you enter, first say, 'Peace to this household.' ⁶ If a person of peace is there, your peace will rest on him; but if not, it will return to you. ⁷ Remain in the same house, eating and drinking what they offer, for the worker is worthy of his wages. Don't move from house to house. ⁸ When you enter any town, and they welcome you, eat the things set before you. ⁹ **Heal the sick who are there, and tell them, 'The kingdom of God has come near you.'**

TRAVELING LIGHT [V. 4]

As you read Jesus' directions, one fact should be clear: our mission is urgent. His emphasis on traveling light amplifies this point. Kingdom work is important and should be done with urgency and intentionality.

PHYSICAL AND SPIRITUAL NEEDS [V. 9]

Jesus' directions show care for both physical and spiritual needs. The disciples were to heal the sick and proclaim the kingdom.

As we continue this study, it's important to notice the dynamic between physical and spiritual needs in Jesus' ministry. We too should be concerned with both physical and spiritual needs.

EXAMINE

Gain a deeper appreciation for what the biblical text says.

Reread the following verse:

LUKE 10:2

² He told them, "The harvest is abundant, but the workers are few. Therefore, pray to the Lord of the harvest to send out workers into his harvest.

Who's the Lord of the harvest? What does this reality teach us about the nature of the task God has given us?

Why don't we often pray for workers in the harvest?

What does the disproportionate ratio of the harvest to the workers tell us about our commitment to God's work in the world? What are we missing?

APPLY

Recognize that the Bible calls us to obey God and to respond to Him with our lives.

Would you stop right now and pray for God to send more workers like Maya, Ben, Aaron, and others David mentioned into the harvest fields?

Would you commit to reaching out to a pastor or a church leader to explore how you could partner with the church to use your gifts in your community or around the world? Set a time and a place for this conversation.

Would you commit to pray every day for the next week and ask God where He might be willing to send you, whether across the street or around the world?

PRAY

Respond to God with praise, thanksgiving, confession, and obedience.

Record a prayer to God in light of today's reading.

PERSONAL STUDY 3

READ

Slowly and intentionally read the Scriptures.

READ LUKE 12:22-34.

LUKE 12:22-30

²² Then he said to his disciples: "Therefore I tell you, **don't worry** about your life, what you will eat; or about the body, what you will wear. ²³ For life is more than food and the body more than clothing. ²⁴ Consider the ravens: They don't sow or reap; they don't have a storeroom or a barn; yet God feeds them. Aren't you worth much more than the birds? ²⁵ Can any of you add one moment to his life span by worrying? ²⁶ If then you're not able to do even a little thing, why worry about the rest?

²⁷ "Consider how the wildflowers grow: They don't labor or spin thread. Yet I tell you, not even Solomon in all his splendor was adorned like one of these. ²⁸ If that's how God clothes the grass, which is in the field today and is thrown into the furnace tomorrow, how much more will he do for you — you of little faith? ²⁹ Don't strive for what you should eat and what you should drink, and don't be anxious. ³⁰ For the **Gentile world** eagerly seeks all these things, and your Father knows that you need them.

■ TWO WAYS OF LIFE

ANXIETY

Teaching these truths as an aside to His disciples (see v. 22), Jesus presented two ways of life—one consumed with worry and the other satisfied in contentment. One reason we have such a hard time being generous toward others is that we're worried about what belongs to us. When we worry about our possessions, our life becomes a shadow of the life God desires for us. Our life is about more than material gain. True life is found in being rich toward God.

■ CONTEXT

GENTILES [V. 30]

To underscore His point, Jesus mentioned that people who know the one true God shouldn't be concerned about the same things Gentiles (those who don't know God) worry about. If God, in His kindness, meets their needs, how much more will He provide for those who know Him and earnestly seek to live a life that pleases Him? As we saw earlier in this study, Jesus often argued from lesser to greater to make a point.

LUKE 12:31-34

³¹ "But seek his kingdom, and these things will be provided for you. ³² Don't be afraid, little flock, because your Father delights to give you the kingdom. ³³ Sell your possessions and give to the poor. Make money-bags for yourselves that won't grow old, an inexhaustible treasure in heaven, where no thief comes near and no moth destroys. ³⁴ **For where your treasure is, there your heart will be also.**

TWO WAYS OF LIFE

CONTENTMENT [V. 31]

Disciples of Jesus can rest in contentment, knowing that what Jesus promises is better than what the world offers.

Jesus assures His disciples that following Him means we'll inherit a kingdom that's infinitely greater than the earthly kingdom we inhabit now. The treasures of Christ's kingdom aren't susceptible to theft or corrosion.

What's more, our Father delights to give us the kingdom. Regardless of our circumstances, we can live with the contentment Paul described in Philippians 4:12, which is far more valuable than any earthly treasure.

KEY VERSE

LUKE 12:34

Jesus understood the direct connection between our hearts and our treasure. We pursue what we love. Where we decide to use our gifts reveals the state of our hearts. This truth reveals why it's important for us to evaluate the ways we're using the resources God has given us.

EXAMINE

Gain a deeper appreciation for what the biblical text says.

What analogies did Jesus use to teach us why we should be free of anxiety and full of contentment?

Why are our hearts and our treasures so closely linked? What does your heart reveal about your treasure?

Jesus' directions are simple, but we often find them hard to obey. Why?

APPLY

Recognize that the Bible calls us to obey God and to respond to Him with our lives.

Evaluate your life. Would you say you're anxious or content? What's the source of your anxiety or contentment?

How could cultivating godly contentment help you be generous toward others and use your gifts to serve others?

What are the specific concerns you worry about that keep you from focusing on the kingdom? Confess these to another believer and ask him or her to hold you accountable in cultivating contentment and confidence in God's provision.

PRAY

Respond to God with praise, thanksgiving, confession, and obedience.

Record a prayer to God in light of today's reading.

Counting the Cost

START

Welcome to session 6 of Something Needs to Change. *Use these questions to begin the conversation.*

> Last week you were asked to consider how God could use your talents for His glory. What excited you about considering the possibilities?

Following Jesus requires much from us. As we heard in the previous session, going where God calls might mean leaving a job we love to serve God in another place around the world.

An underlying theme in all of these accounts in Luke is the cost of gospel obedience. This week we're going to focus on an idea that many of us don't think about enough: the cost of following Jesus.

> Do you know someone who has paid a price to follow Jesus? Share that story.

Ask someone to pray. Then watch the video, "Day 6: Counting the Cost." Encourage group members to follow along, using the participant guide on pages 183–84 or at LifeWay.com/SomethingNeedstoChange.

To access video sessions, subscribe to SmallGroup.com or visit LifeWay.com/SomethingNeedstoChange.

DISCUSS

Use these questions to discuss the video teaching in your group.

How many sermons have you heard about following Jesus? How many address the cost of following Jesus? Why is this a topic we don't often talk about?

Almost absent from any call to follow Jesus today is the cost of that call. In the first century, it was costly to follow Jesus. People lost respect, family, and even their lives. For millions of people all over the world today, it's still costly to follow Jesus. The cost for you may be different or more subtle, but Scripture is clear: following Jesus should cost you something.

Refer to Luke 14:25-33 for the following questions.

Does it surprise you that this was an initial invitation to follow Jesus? Why do we think this kind of obedience is advanced Christianity, reserved for the spiritually mature?

How would people in the first century have heard Jesus' call to bear a cross? What does it mean for us, as David said, to follow Jesus on His terms?

Read Galatians 2:20. How does a relationship with Jesus Christ change everything about us?

We're constantly tempted to follow Jesus on our own terms rather than His. We mistakenly believe this kind of Christianity is only for serious, fully mature Christians. In reality, this is basic Christianity. There are no tiers of disciples. Jesus requires the same kind of obedience from all who follow Him.

To be clear, we shouldn't seek persecution or hardship, but we have to be willing to put everything on the line for Jesus—our possessions, plans, dreams, and desires—and say, "Jesus, it's all Yours. How do You want me to use it? Where do You want me to live? I'll do whatever You want me to do." The cost is great, but the reward is greater.

Read Matthew 13:44. What's the reward for following Jesus? How have you experienced this reward?

What makes the cost of following Jesus worth it? Why should we sacrifice everything to follow Him?

Passages like Luke 14:25-33 make sense only when we realize that Jesus is supremely satisfying. He's the treasure in a field worth selling everything to pursue. This reality is why we obey. We could never do enough to earn favor with Jesus. On the cross Jesus did everything necessary for us to know Him and follow Him.

What in your life do you find yourself holding on to rather than giving to Jesus?

PRAYER

Jesus, thank You for paying the ultimate cost so that we could know You. Help us be bold and courageous in our witness, willing to go anywhere and do anything You ask so that Your name can be made known in all the earth.

As you close, remind the group to complete the three personal studies that follow. Encourage them to spend time thinking about the suggestions for getting involved, located on the back of the participant guide.

THE KINGDOM OF HEAVEN

is like treasure, buried in a field, that a man found and reburied. Then in his joy he goes and sells everything he has and buys that field.

MATTHEW 13:44

REFLECTIONS

Spiritual Warfare

After packing up my things, I make my way to the teahouse, where I sit down at the breakfast table next to Chris and Nabin and across from Aaron and Sigs. As we eat our usual morning meal, Chris asks me what I was reading in my Bible that morning. I share about the end of Luke 14 and the importance of counting the cost of following Christ in this world, like a builder preparing to construct a tower or a king preparing to go to war.

Then I ask Aaron, "When you decided to give your life doing ministry in these mountains, how did you count that cost? How did you measure what ministry here was going to take?"

"That's a great question," Aaron says. "We knew that physically, work in these mountains would be hard for obvious reasons. But we learned very quickly that the physical challenges were nothing compared to the spiritual challenges. When we first came up to these villages and started sharing the gospel, we were immediately told to leave and never come back. In fact, a few people threatened to kill us if we tried to come back."

"Why?" I ask.

"There's a strong belief here that you need to appease various gods or spirits in order for things to go well for you. And if anyone disrupts the stability of worship for those gods or spirits, then bad things can happen. As a result, when people found out that we were followers of Jesus, they believed we were introducing a foreign, competing God who would upset their gods, so they wanted us gone.

"And you know," Aaron goes on, "there's a sense in which they were exactly right. Based on what the Bible says about spiritual warfare, there's absolutely a false god named the devil who has been deceiving minds and hearts for centuries in these mountains. He has kept Jesus from being proclaimed as the one true God here for generations, and he will do whatever he can to keep that from changing."

Aaron pauses as if he's reluctant to share something. I can tell something specific is on his mind, so I ask him, "How have you seen that spiritual warfare play out?"

He takes a deep breath and says, "Let me tell you a story that I probably wouldn't believe if I hadn't been a part of it. But it will give you some perspective on the spiritual war that's waging in these mountains.

"One day," Aaron starts, "I was hiking through a village not far from here. It was early in my time up here, and it was my first time ever to be in that particular village. As I was hiking, all of a sudden a woman, maybe in her midthirties, came running past me really fast. She startled me because she seemed out of control, and I could sense that something was wrong with her. She ran ahead, though, and I lost sight of her.

"A few minutes later," Aaron continues, "the trail led me right next to where this woman's house was apparently located. As I got near the house, suddenly I saw this same woman dart out the front door. She had a crazed look on her face and a bottle in her hand, which I later found out was insecticide. She stood there in front of her door facing me as I walked toward her on the trail, and she started shouting. I stopped in my tracks, totally stunned and unsure of what was happening.

"That's when the woman yelled in the local dialect, 'This is your welcome to our villages,' and she took the bottle in her hand and started drinking it. I didn't know what was in the bottle, but I immediately got concerned when her husband came running out of the house with their kids, all yelling, 'No! No! No!' But by the time they got to her, she had swallowed almost everything in the bottle. At that point she started convulsing and gasping for breath. The husband started yelling for help, so I dropped my pack and ran straight to them. She seemed to be losing consciousness, and before long she wasn't breathing. I started trying to revive her, but nothing was working. Within a matter of minutes she was dead."

We sit silently at the breakfast table, trying to imagine this scene.

"It was one of the worst moments of my entire life," Aaron says. "To see a woman kill herself in front of her husband and children. And to do it because I came hiking into this village."

"How do you know it was because of you?" I ask. "Did you even know this woman?"

"No," Aaron answers, "I'd never been in this village, and I'd never met this woman. The first time I ever saw her was when she came running past me on the trail."

Aaron pauses again and then continues. "That's when I knew that the physical battles of hunger and sickness in these villages pale in comparison to the spiritual battle for people's hearts and minds. And I had to ask the question 'Was I ready for that kind of battle?' "

As Chris asks Aaron more questions, my mind immediately goes to whether God is calling me to work in these mountains. *Am I ready for this kind of spiritual war?* I wonder. And not just me. I think about all the opportunities we discussed yesterday for students, professionals, and retirees to spread the gospel around the world. Indeed, that's no light commitment. Like a king preparing for war, there's a cost to be counted.

This is a real story about a real family. Spend some time praying for the spiritual warfare in this region of the world.

PERSONAL STUDY 1

READ

Slowly and intentionally read the Scriptures.

READ LUKE 14:25-27.

Although we looked at this section of Scripture during the group session, these strong words from Jesus merit further consideration. Following Jesus means counting the cost of discipleship.

LUKE 14:25-27

²⁵ Now great crowds were traveling with him. So he turned and said to them: ²⁶ "If anyone comes to me and **does not hate** his own father and mother, wife and children, brothers and sisters — yes, and even his own life — he cannot be my disciple. ²⁷ Whoever does not **bear his own cross** and come after me cannot be my disciple.

■ LITERARY CONTEXT [V. 26]

The first condition for discipleship that Jesus established is a disciple should hate his or her family. Jesus didn't mean a disciple should literally hate his or her family. He used the word *hate* rhetorically to compare the affection we have for our family with the affection we have for Him. He was saying our relationship with Him should make our familial relationships look like hate.

■ HISTORICAL CONTEXT

THE CROSS [V. 27]

Jesus' second condition was to bear a cross. Though we wear crosses around our necks and hang them on our walls, no one in the first century would have done such a thing. Crucifixion was the preferred method of Roman capital punishment. A first-century person would have responded to a cross the way contemporary people respond to an electric chair or to a lethal injection. Furthermore, to a Jewish audience, the cross was an incredible offense, for someone who hung on a tree was considered cursed by God (see Deut. 21:23).

■ THE COST OF DISCIPLESHIP

The New Testament is filled with teachings on the cost of discipleship. Consider the following verses.

VERSE	COST
Matthew 10:38; 16:24; Mark 8:34; Luke 9:23; 14:27	Take up your cross.
Matthew 8:19-20; Luke 9:57-58	Jesus has no place to lay His head.
Romans 14:7	Die to yourself.
Matthew 8:21-22; Luke 9:59-60	Embrace unqualified commitment to Jesus.
2 Corinthians 5:15	Live for Jesus.
Galatians 2:20	You're crucified with Christ.
Luke 14:33	Forsake possessions.
Philippians 3:7-8	Suffer the loss of all things.
John 15:20; Acts 14:22; 2 Timothy 3:12	Expect persecution.
John 12:25	Lose your life.

EXAMINE

Gain a deeper appreciation for what the biblical text says.

Read some of the verses about the cost of discipleship in the chart on the previous page. Why do the Gospels prioritize this imperative?

What does it mean, in practical terms, to bear a cross?

How might a first-century audience have responded to Jesus' calls to costly obedience? How might a twenty-first-century person respond to the same call?

APPLY

Recognize that the Bible calls us to obey God and to respond to Him with our lives.

Evaluate your affection for Jesus. What's keeping you from loving Him supremely?

What might Jesus be asking you to give up in order to follow Him more closely?

Read John 15:13. What did Jesus sacrifice on your behalf? How does Jesus' supreme love for you motivate your sacrifice for Him?

PRAY

Respond to God with praise, thanksgiving, confession, and obedience.

Record a prayer to God in light of today's reading.

PERSONAL STUDY 2

READ

Slowly and intentionally read the Scriptures.

READ LUKE 14:28-35.

Today's reading further explains the teaching of Jesus we examined yesterday. Through Jesus' examples we gain a clearer understanding of what it means to follow Him.

LUKE 14:28-33

> [28] "Which of you, wanting to build a tower, doesn't first sit down and calculate the cost to see if he has enough to complete it? [29] Otherwise, after he has laid the foundation and cannot finish it, all the onlookers will begin to ridicule him, [30] saying, 'This man started to build and wasn't able to finish.' [31] **Or what king**, going to war against another king, will not first sit down and decide if he is able with ten thousand to oppose the one who comes against him with twenty thousand? [32] If not, while the other is still far off, he sends a delegation and asks for terms of peace. [33] In the same way, therefore, every one of you who does not renounce all his possessions cannot be my disciple.

■ ILLUSTRATIONS

A TOWER AND A KING

The third condition that Jesus placed on discipleship in Luke 14 was to renounce all. He explained this requirement by using two stories: the first of a man seeking to build a tower, the second of a king going to war.

A man who built a tower without determining how much it cost would have been supremely foolish. A king similarly needed to determine the cost of a war before making the decision to fight. The point of both examples is clear: discipleship requires a full-hearted commitment to the task. Followers of Jesus are to be undivided in their purpose.

LUKE 14:34-35

³⁴ "Now, **salt** is good, but if salt should lose its taste, how will it be made salty? ³⁵ It isn't fit for the soil or for the manure pile; they throw it out. Let anyone who has ears to hear listen."

■ ILLUSTRATIONS

SALT [V. 34]

Salt in the ancient world was impure compared to the salt used today. As a result, it quickly lost its taste. Salt that doesn't taste salty isn't good for any use. It's worth less than manure, which can be used to grow plants. Jesus was saying a disciple who hasn't embraced the cost isn't useful in the kingdom. These words should sober us.

■ MAIN POINT

The last example of salt ties together all the teaching in this passage. Jesus was saying that those who don't meet these costs of discipleship aren't fit to be His disciples. Though we might tend to see the level of sacrifice Jesus was asking for in this teaching as descriptive of advanced Christianity, this level of commitment is Christianity 101.

EXAMINE

Gain a deeper appreciation for what the biblical text says.

When you read Jesus' examples of counting the cost, how could you restate them for a modern audience?

What's the difficult truth that underlies all three examples?

Why do we omit the call to costly obedience from our gospel presentations?

APPLY

Recognize that the Bible calls us to obey God and to respond to Him with our lives.

Read Luke 14:34-35 again.

Now, salt is good, but if salt should lose its taste, how will it be made salty? It isn't fit for the soil or for the manure pile; they throw it out. Let anyone who has ears to hear listen.

Why do we often believe that the kind of discipleship Jesus requires is only for supermature Christians?

What challenges you about the call to forsake everything and follow Jesus?

PRAY

Respond to God with praise, thanksgiving, confession, and obedience.

Record a prayer to God in light of today's reading.

PERSONAL STUDY 3

READ

Slowly and intentionally read the Scriptures.

READ LUKE 18:18-30.

Today we'll examine a well-known incident from Jesus' ministry involving the rich young ruler. This story appears in three of the four Gospels (see Matt. 19:16-30; Mark 10:17-31; Luke 18:18-30). Here we see a man unwilling to pay the cost of following Jesus.

LUKE 18:18-23

18 A **ruler** asked him, "Good teacher, what must I do to inherit eternal life?"

19 "Why do you call me good?" Jesus asked him. "No one is good except God alone. 20 You know the commandments: Do not commit adultery; do not murder; do not steal; do not bear false witness; honor your father and mother."

21 "I have kept all these from my youth," he said.

22 When Jesus heard this, he told him, "You still lack one thing: **Sell all you have and distribute it to the poor**, and you will have treasure in heaven. Then come, follow me."

23 After he heard this, he became extremely sad, because he was very rich.

■ LOOKING DEEPER

RULER [V. 18]

Luke often used the word translated *ruler* in his Gospel to refer to Pharisees or other religious leaders. Matthew's Gospel provides the additional detail that the man was young (see 19:22). It's possible that he was either a leader in the synagogue or an influential man known for his wealth and religious devotion. You likely know many people today who fit this description.

■ RESPONSE

A REVEALING COMMENT

The young man asked Jesus a good question that many people ask: "What must I do to inherit eternal life?" (Luke 18:18). Because the young man asked in terms of doing, Jesus answered in terms of doing. Jesus challenged him to keep the Ten Commandments. Although the young man believed he had kept the law perfectly, his answer showed that he had failed to measure himself against God's standard because he believed his works would merit eternal life. In response Jesus issued another challenge: "Sell all you have and distribute it to the poor" (v. 22). This command was too much for the man. He went away sad because he was unwilling to embrace the cost of following Jesus.

■ LITERARY CONTEXT

HYPERBOLE [V. 25]

In verse 25 Jesus intentionally exaggerated to make His point. He wasn't condemning wealthy people; it's possible to be greedy whether someone is rich or poor. Jesus was pointing out that being entangled with the things of earth will keep us from heaven. This fact is the reason He added, "What is impossible with man is possible with God" (v. 27).

LUKE 18:24-30

24 Seeing that he became sad, Jesus said, "How hard it is for those who have wealth to enter the kingdom of God! 25 For it is easier for a **camel to go through the eye** of a needle than for a rich person to enter the kingdom of God."

26 Those who heard this asked, "Then who can be saved?"

27 He replied, "What is impossible with man is possible with God."

28 Then Peter said, "Look, we have left what we had and followed you."

29 So he said to them, "Truly I tell you, there is no one who has left a house, wife or brothers or sisters, parents or children because of the kingdom of God, 30 who will not receive many times more at this time, and **eternal life in the age to come**."

■ CONTEXT

RICHES AND BLESSING

In the first-century world, material riches were seen as a sign of God's approval. Those who heard Jesus' words were perplexed (see v. 26) because His teaching ran against the conventional philosophy of the culture. The Gospel writers were showing that the oppressed and materially poor have access to blessings that the rich find a much harder time uncovering.

■ RESULTS

TREASURES IN HEAVEN [V. 30]

For a disciple of Jesus, the reward of service isn't found on earth but in heaven. When you're called to sacrifice for the sake of following Jesus, you'll gain more than you'll lose. At the end of life, no one wishes they had accumulated more stuff.

EXAMINE

Gain a deeper appreciation for what the biblical text says.

Look more closely at verses Luke 18:29-30. Circle what Jesus promises to those who forsake the comforts of this life to follow Him.

He said to them, "Truly I tell you, there is no one who has left a house, wife or brothers or sisters, parents or children because of the kingdom of God, who will not receive many times more at this time, and eternal life in the age to come."

Why is the reward Jesus offers for following Him more valuable than the things of earth we give up to pursue Him?

Compare this day's reading to the readings for days 1 and 2. How are they similar?

APPLY

Recognize that the Bible calls us to obey God and to respond to Him with our lives.

What characteristics of the rich young ruler do you see in yourself?

What do you have the hardest time giving up in order to follow Jesus? Why?

What has God taught you this week about the cost of following Him?

PRAY

Respond to God with praise, thanksgiving, confession, and obedience.

Record a prayer in light of today's reading. Spend time asking God what you need to relinquish in order to follow Him more freely.

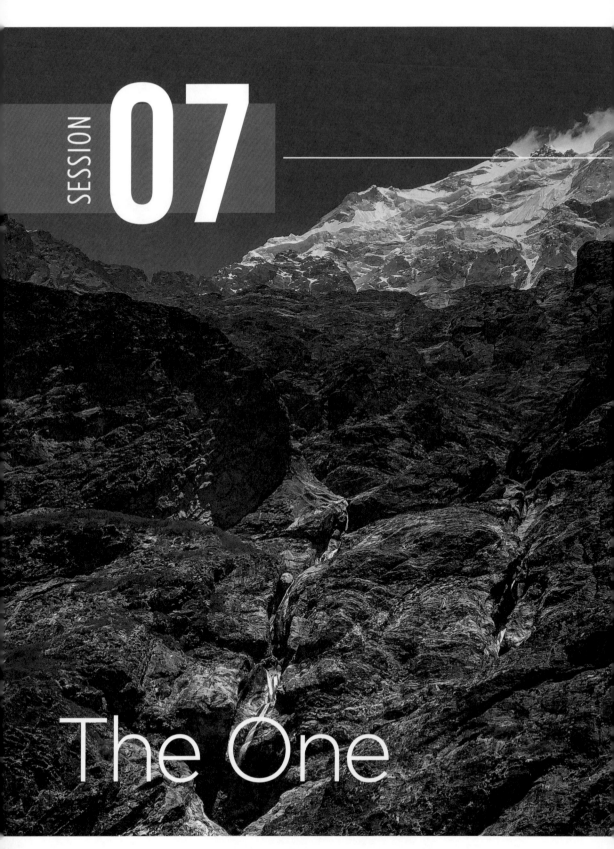

07

The One

START

Welcome to session 7 of Something Needs to Change. *Use these questions to begin the conversation.*

Last week you considered the cost of following Jesus. Is this topic something you had ever thought about before? What did you learn about following Jesus?

When you understand how deeply Jesus loves you, you'll be compelled to do whatever it takes to make Him known in the world. As other people respond to the call to follow Christ, we join the celebration of heaven as men and women from every tribe and nation give their lives to Jesus. This is the goal of the church.

Have you ever been present when someone believed the gospel for the first time? What was that experience like?

Ask someone to pray. Then watch the video, "Day 7: The One." Encourage group members to follow along, using the participant guide on pages 185–86 or at LifeWay.com/SomethingNeedstoChange.

To access video sessions, subscribe to SmallGroup.com or visit LifeWay.com/SomethingNeedstoChange.

DISCUSS

Use these questions to discuss the video teaching in your group.

Refer to Luke 15 for the following questions.

Look at verses 1-3. What caused Jesus to tell these three parables? What did the Pharisees misunderstand about the kingdom?

What's the most significant takeaway from all three parables?

The point of these three parables is clear: God is passionate about the one who's far from Him. Heaven erupts in praise when one person, cut off from God, is reconciled to Him in love (see v. 10). To be like Jesus is to long for people to know Him.

If bringing sinners to faith in Christ makes heaven rejoice, why do we give much of our time, attention, and efforts to lesser things?

How do we maintain focus on important priorities without missing the most important priority?

Our priorities should be God's priorities. God has a universe to run, galaxies to uphold, governments to rule, and more than seven billion people to sustain, yet He still cares about the one personally and intimately. The gospel requires that we reconsider our priorities and give up good pursuits in order to more fully pursue what makes heaven rejoice. This is the reason we embrace the hardship required to take the gospel to the nations.

David mentioned that visiting the Himalayas helped shift his perspective because once he heard the people's stories and learned their names, he couldn't ignore their need. People are easier to forget if you don't know their names.

How does personally knowing unbelieving or needy people change the way we see our call to share the gospel?

Read Romans 10:14-15. What does it look like to live in a way that makes heaven rejoice?

God wants people to know Him, and in His wisdom He chose us to share that message to the ends of the earth. God could have orchestrated this mission in any manner He chose, yet He loves us enough to invite us into His work. Because God is passionate about the one, let's live to be passionate about the one.

What changes about your perception of yourself when you realize that God loves you as He loves the one?

Think of ways you could make more room in your schedule in order to spend more time around people who need the gospel—both at home and around the world. How could we encourage one another in this pursuit?

PRAYER

Father, thank You for Your passion for the one. Please give us hearts for people who don't know You. We ask that Your kingdom would come and Your will would be done through this group as it is in heaven. God, glorify Your name in this community and around the world and use us to accomplish Your mission. You don't need our help, but we delight to be a small part of what You're doing to bring people to Yourself.

As you close, remind the group to complete the three personal studies that follow. Encourage them to spend time thinking about the suggestions for getting involved, located on the back of the participant guide.

The Son of Man
has come to
SEEK AND
TO SAVE
THE LOST.

LUKE 19:10

REFLECTIONS

One Is Found

I roll up my sleeping bag and stuff it into my pack one last time, at least for this trek. It's hard to believe only one week has gone by, because I feel I've experienced a year's worth of encounters the past few days.

As Aaron warned, the temperature rises as we hike, and soon I'm sweating. Six days ago I was so cold I couldn't imagine ever sweating again. Now I start shedding layers for the final leg of the trek.

The scenery is different too. When we began six days ago, all the terrain was white. Now lush greens and bright browns color the landscape. It's beautiful in an entirely new way. We're following the river, walking back and forth across it on suspended steel bridges. The floors of the bridges are grated, so you can see the water rushing over rapids far below. Some bridges are sturdier than others, and some of them shake and sway when a strong wind gust hits.

As I walk, I start to reminisce about the week. I wonder how I'm going to summarize for Heather and the kids all I've experienced. I feel as if any attempt to describe it all will be woefully inadequate. Still I can't wait to see them and give it a try.

But more experiences are still to come. As we approach the trailhead, Aaron tells us that before we board the bus, we'll quickly stop at two places. The first is a center for children with disabilities. Specifically, we're going to meet a teenager named Malkit.

Malkit, we soon learn, has cerebral palsy, which affects his muscle coordination, vision, hearing, speech, and ability to swallow food. Malkit was born in one of the villages we walked through this week. When he was ten years old, he was found chained in a barn by Nabin, our translator.

Malkit's family thought he was cursed and didn't know how to care for him, so he grew up with the animals in the barn. When Nabin found him, he didn't know how to walk. Nabin, having been chained in a barn once himself, immediately began working to rescue Malkit. With the support of Malkit's family, Nabin and Aaron brought him down the mountain, and along with many others, they shared God's love with him. Not long ago they helped him settle in at this center, where he has care for his unique needs.

As we walk in, Malkit sees Aaron and Nabin, and a contagious smile sweeps his face. He's full of joy as he slowly walks (yes, he's walking now!) to Aaron and Nabin and gives them both huge hugs. Malkit starts sharing through slurred speech how thankful he is for the way these men shared and showed God's love to him. He also says how much he enjoys living at this center, the friends he has, and all the things he's able to do, including physical therapy and all kinds of group activities and games.

Here's a young man who was once chained in a barn, living with animals, unable to walk, with no one to help him. Now he's smiling and walking and playing and hugging and laughing. And best of all, he knows God loves him.

I smile as I watch Aaron and Nabin interact with Malkit. Here's a young man who was once chained in a barn, living with animals, unable to walk, with no one to help him. Now he's smiling and walking and playing and hugging and laughing. And best of all, he knows God loves him enough to send Jesus to make it possible for him to have eternal life.

Indeed, there's a lot to celebrate when, in a Luke 15 way, one who was lost has been found.

How does Malkit's story highlight the need to seek the one?

PERSONAL STUDY 1

READ

Slowly and intentionally read the Scriptures.

READ LUKE 15:1-7.

For the next three days we'll take a closer look at Luke 15 to examine God's specific care for the one. If God longs to see one sinner come to know Him in love, so must we. The first few verses of this passage give us helpful context.

LUKE 15:1-2

15 All the **tax collectors and sinners** were approaching to listen to him. ² And the Pharisees and scribes were **complaining**, "This man welcomes sinners and eats with them."

■ HISTORICAL CONTEXT

TAX COLLECTORS AND SINNERS [V. 1]

Tax collectors weren't well regarded by Jews in the first century because of their partnership with the Roman government. To make a living, tax collectors resorted to extortion and dishonesty in collecting their debts; therefore, other Jews saw them as traitors and hated them. *Sinners* is a broader term, but in this context it likely refers to people who didn't keep the purity commands in the eyes of the Pharisees.

■ TAKE NOTICE

GRUMBLING PHARISEES [V. 2]

On face value the Pharisees' comment could have been one of earnest wonder. However, Luke's added commentary lets us know they were complaining. The religious teachers took great pains to separate themselves from such people. Jesus' close relationship with sinners was unthinkable and offensive to them.

Jesus not only welcomed sinners but also ate with them. Sharing a meal with sinners was a tacit statement about their value and worth. Jesus came to help sinners. To help sinners, you have to get to know them.

■ HISTORICAL CONTEXT

SHEPHERDS

The flock would have been the shepherds' livelihood and their chief concern. A shepherd with three hundred sheep would have been considered prosperous. The shepherd in this parable, who had only one hundred sheep, would have been a man of modest means.

LUKE 15:3-7

³ He told them this parable: ⁴ "What man among you, who has a hundred sheep and loses one of them, **does not leave the ninety-nine in the open field** and go after the lost one until he finds it? ⁵ When he has found it, he joyfully puts it on his shoulders, ⁶ and coming home, he calls his friends and neighbors together, saying to them, 'Rejoice with me, because I have found my lost sheep!' ⁷ I tell you, in the same way, there will be more joy in heaven over one sinner who repents than over ninety-nine righteous people who don't need repentance.

■ TAKEAWAYS

WHAT DO WE LEARN ABOUT GOD FROM THIS PARABLE?

In this parable the shepherd represents God. By observing the shepherd, we can learn about God.

1. The shepherd left ninety-nine sheep that were safe and accounted for in light of his concern for the one, while he gave the lost sheep special attention.
2. When he found the sheep, he put it on his shoulders because a sheep lost in open pasture would have been weak and tired. The care the shepherd provided the found sheep illustrates God's tender, protective care for His sheep.
3. The shepherd shared with his friends and neighbors the good news that the sheep had been found. He was filled with celebration and joy as the one was folded back into the ninety-nine.
4. The joy of the shepherd couldn't compare with the joy in heaven. Jesus said there's more rejoicing in heaven when a sinner comes to faith in Christ than over the many who don't need to be saved. Heaven celebrates the return of the lost.

EXAMINE

Gain a deeper appreciation for what the biblical text says.

What word did the scribes and Pharisees use to describe Jesus' relationship with sinners? What do Jesus' actions teach us about Him? About other people?

Think about the statement "This man welcomes sinners" (v. 2). Why is this such an incredible and inflammatory statement?

What care did the shepherd exercise when he found the lost sheep?

APPLY

Recognize that the Bible calls us to obey God and to respond to Him with our lives.

Is your relationship with "tax collectors and sinners" (v. 1) more like that of Jesus or more like that of the religious leaders?

What changes about our desire to share the gospel when we see people who are far away from God not as a burden but as people who need to be reconciled to the God who loves them?

The shepherd who found the lost sheep integrated the found one back into the flock. How can we ensure that our church is a flock that welcomes lost sheep into the fold?

PRAY

Respond to God with praise, thanksgiving, confession, and obedience.

Record a prayer to God in light of today's reading.

PERSONAL STUDY 2

READ

Slowly and intentionally read the Scriptures.

READ LUKE 15:8-10.

Jesus continued His series of parables. Whereas the first parable featured one sheep lost among one hundred, this parable features one coin lost among ten. Jesus intentionally limited the scope of the search.

LUKE 15:8-10

8 "Or what woman who has ten silver coins, if she loses one coin, does not light a lamp, sweep the house, and search carefully until she finds it? 9 When she finds it, she calls her friends and neighbors together, saying, 'Rejoice with me, because I have found the silver coin I lost!' 10 I tell you, in the same way, there is joy in the presence of God's angels over one sinner who repents."

■ DISTINCTION

THE SEARCH

Compared to the first parable, the search for the missing item is described in much more detail. The woman lit a lamp because houses often had no windows. She then used a broom to check under the edges of furniture and in dark corners. Jesus said she carefully searched until the coin was found. The message to us should be clear: we're to be diligent in our pursuit of the lost.

■ HISTORICAL CONTEXT
COINS [V. 8]

The coin that was lost was a drachma. This amount would have been about a day's wages for an average laborer—a modest sum of money.

■ THE RESULTS
REJOICING [V. 9]

ON EARTH. After recovering her coin, like the shepherd, the woman gathered people near to share in the joy that came from finding what was lost. The joy illustrates the value of what was lost.

IN HEAVEN. Once again the parable ends with rejoicing over the recovery of what was lost. Jesus said, "There is joy in the presence of God's angels" (v. 10) over the one.

EXAMINE

Gain a deeper appreciation for what the biblical text says.

What does the woman's search teach us about the importance of what was lost?

What's similar and what's different between this parable and the one told in verses 3-7?

Why did the woman want other people to rejoice with her? When was the last time you invited someone to participate in your joy?

APPLY

Recognize that the Bible calls us to obey God and to respond to Him with our lives.

How diligently are you searching for the lost?

Whom do you know who can encourage you and celebrate with you as you seek to engage people with the gospel?

Why should the joy of God fuel our desire to reach the lost?

PRAY

Respond to God with praise, thanksgiving, confession, and obedience.

Record a prayer to God in light of today's reading.

PERSONAL STUDY 3

READ

Slowly and intentionally read the Scriptures.

READ LUKE 15:11-32.

The last parable in Luke 15 is the best known of the three—the parable of the prodigal son. Here Jesus took the search from one out of a hundred and one out of ten to one out of one. A second son figures in the parable, but the primary focus is on the lost son.

LUKE 15:11-19

11 He also said: "A man had two sons. 12 The younger of them said to his father, **'Father, give me the share of the estate I have coming to me.'** So he distributed the assets to them. 13 Not many days later, the younger son gathered together all he had and traveled to a distant country, where he **squandered** his estate in foolish living. 14 After he had spent everything, a severe famine struck that country, and he had nothing. 15 Then he went to work for one of the citizens of that country, who sent him into his fields to feed pigs. 16 He longed to eat his fill from the pods that the pigs were eating, but no one would give him anything. 17 When he came to his senses, he said, 'How many of my father's hired workers have more than enough food, and here I am dying of hunger! 18 I'll get up, go to my father, and say to him, "Father, I have sinned against heaven and in your sight. 19 I'm no longer worthy to be called your son. Make me like one of your hired workers."'

■ HISTORICAL CONTEXT

INHERITANCE [V. 12]

By approaching His father and asking for His inheritance, the son was effectively saying to His Father, "I wish you were dead." To make this scenario even more unusual, the father honored the request and gave the younger son his share of the inheritance. The younger son's inheritance would have been one third of the father's estate.

■ WORD STUDY

SQUANDERED AND FOOLISH [V. 13]

The word translated *squandered* in verse 13 literally means "to scatter or disperse." The picture here is of someone throwing away all he has. *Foolish* means "wasteful." Taken together, these words provide a portrait of a young man in full rebellion, uninterested in what mattered to his father.

LUKE 15:20-32

²⁰ So he got up and went to his father. But while the son was still a long way off, **his father saw him and was filled with compassion. He ran, threw his arms around his neck, and kissed him.** ²¹ The son said to him, 'Father, I have sinned against heaven and in your sight. I'm no longer worthy to be called your son.'

²² "But the father told his servants, 'Quick! Bring out the best robe and put it on him; put a ring on his finger and sandals on his feet. ²³ Then bring the fattened calf and slaughter it, and let's celebrate with a feast, ²⁴ because this son of mine was dead and is alive again; he was lost and is found!' So they began to celebrate.

²⁵ "Now his older son was in the field; as he came near the house, he heard music and dancing. ²⁶ So he summoned one of the servants, questioning what these things meant. ²⁷ 'Your brother is here,' he told him, 'and your father has slaughtered the fattened calf because he has him back safe and sound.'

²⁸ **"Then he became angry** and didn't want to go in. So his father came out and pleaded with him. ²⁹ But he replied to his father, 'Look, I have been slaving many years for you, and I have never disobeyed your orders, yet you never gave me a goat so that I could celebrate with my friends. ³⁰ But when this son of yours came, who has devoured your assets with prostitutes, you slaughtered the fattened calf for him.'

³¹ "'Son,' he said to him, 'you are always with me, and everything I have is yours. ³² But we had to celebrate and rejoice, because this brother of yours was dead and is alive again; he was lost and is found.'"

■ RESPONSES

THE FATHER

The father's love for his son is evident in his decision to run toward him. As they embraced, the younger son began to rattle off his apology, but the father immediately showered his wayward son with grace, forgiving him and restoring all he had lost. He also threw an extravagant party to welcome the lost son home.

THE OLDER SON

While the father embraced the lost son, the older brother stewed in anger and self-righteousness. Instead of celebrating the return of his brother, he was obsessed with his brother's identity as a sinner. His response to his father outlined his own résumé of obedience. When he mentioned his brother, he called him "this son of yours" (v. 30). Jesus was drawing an intentional contrast between the rejection of the older brother and the welcome of the forgiving father.

EXAMINE

Gain a deeper appreciation for what the biblical text says.

What led to the prodigal's repentance? How do we know it was sincere?

What led the older brother to reject his younger brother? With which brother do you identify more? Why?

What does the father's response teach us about God?

APPLY

Recognize that the Bible calls us to obey God and to respond to Him with our lives.

In what ways is your self-righteousness creating a blind spot that keeps you from rejoicing in the salvation of sinners?

Why should this account give us hope for people who seem far off from God without any sign of coming close to Him?

Where are you seeing God at work to draw people to Himself? How can you celebrate God's redemptive work this week?

PRAY

Respond to God with praise, thanksgiving, confession, and obedience.

Record a prayer to God in light of today's reading. Pray for someone you know in a far-off country.

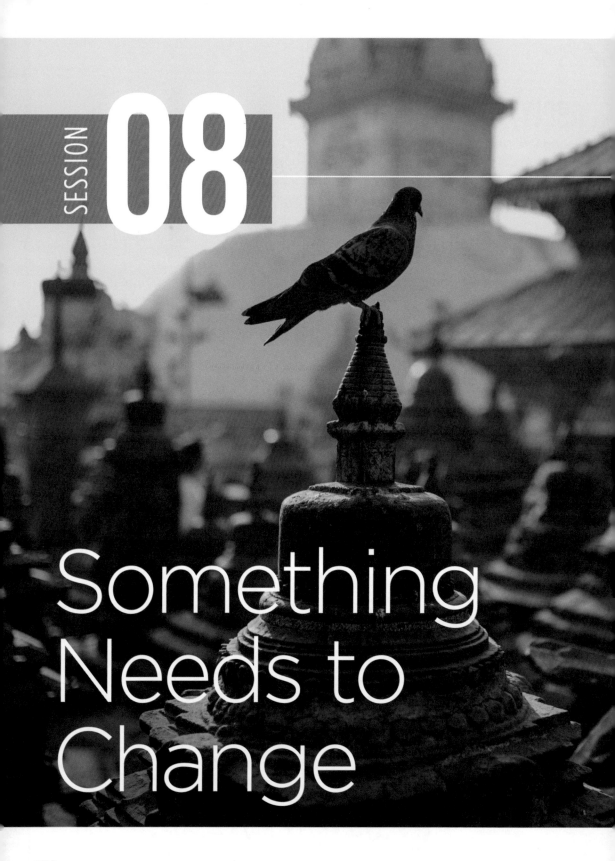

Something Needs to Change

START

Welcome to session 8 of Something Needs to Change. *Use these questions to begin the conversation.*

In the previous session you were challenged to pray specifically for one unbelieving friend. Did you get an opportunity to spend time with that friend? How did that experience go?

What has challenged you most about our study together?

Today we come to the end of our journey. Through our time together we've considered big questions and asked God to work in and through us for the sake of His glory in all nations. To end our study, we're going to address a few final big questions as we consider where God wants us to go from here.

Ask someone to pray. Then watch the video, "Day 8: Something Needs to Change" Encourage group members to follow along, using the participant guide on pages 187–88 or at LifeWay.com/SomethingNeedstoChange.

To access video sessions, subscribe to SmallGroup.com or visit LifeWay.com/SomethingNeedstoChange.

DISCUSS

Use these questions to discuss the video teaching in your group.

In light of urgent physical and spiritual need and for the sake of the two billion people on their way to a Christless eternity, something needs to change about the way we live. Today we're going to spend the bulk of our time considering the questions David asked in the video session.

Refer to Luke 9:57-62 for the following questions.

Are we going to choose comfort, or are we going to choose the cross? How does comfort keep us from pursuing the cross?

Are we going to settle for maintenance, or are we going to sacrifice for mission? David opened by sharing the first time he saw trafficked girls in a city. He confessed that in that moment he wanted to put his head in the sand and pretend what he saw wasn't real. Why is this a normal reaction for us?

Will our lives be marked by indecisive minds or undivided hearts? Why do we hesitate doing what we know the Lord has called us to do?

People who don't know the Lord are entering eternity every day. We simply can't go on with life as usual. We must live with urgency and gospel purpose. We don't have time to sit back and relax. If we aren't careful, we can settle for monotonous spiritual motion, living week by week unconcerned about the mission God has given us.

In the passage we read, Jesus confronted three people. What excuses did they give? What kept them from giving their whole hearts to Jesus?

In what ways do you identity with the people Jesus confronted?

Three people approached Jesus and had the opportunity to follow Him, but they all turned Him down, unwilling to pay the cost. Jesus calls us to choose what's best for the kingdom of God instead of what's best for us. Once we realize what's at stake, we no longer have room to hesitate in our calling. Don't allow the fruit of this study to be indecision and inaction.

Close by reviewing the following challenges and consider ways you can meet them together as a group and as a church. List ideas under each.

1. Work hard to help well amidst earthly suffering.

2. Work hardest to keep people from eternal suffering.

3. Be the church God calls us to be.

4. Run the race God calls you to run.

PRAYER

God, thank You for saving me and calling me to live for the sake of Your name in the world. Help me identity specific areas to which You're calling me and lead me to be open to Your calling in my life.

As you close, remind the group to complete the three personal studies that follow. Encourage them to spend time thinking about the suggestions for getting involved, located on the back of the participant guide.

No one who puts his hand to the plow and looks back is fit for the KINGDOM OF GOD.

LUKE 9:62

REFLECTIONS

Tired of Talking

On the way to the airport, sitting next to Aaron as he drove, I ask him, "Aaron, weren't you the pastor of a church before you moved out here?"

"I was."

"That was after you had that first experience in these mountains, right?"

"Yeah. When I came back down the mountain after meeting that trafficker, I decided I was going to do everything I could to spread the gospel and show God's grace in these mountains. But I didn't immediately move out here. Instead, I pastored a couple of different churches and, as a pastor, I worked to mobilize people for work here. I started building a team—both with people from this country and with churches in other countries."

"That's interesting," I say as I think about my own desire as a pastor to mobilize people for work in different places around the world. "So what made you decide to leave pastoring a church in order to move your family here?"

Aaron smiles and pauses. I can tell he's hesitant to answer, almost as though he doesn't want to say what he's thinking. So I ask again, "Why did you leave pastoring to come here?"

"Do you really want to know?"

"I've asked you twice now," I laugh as I say it. "Yes, I really want to know!"

"I got tired of talking," he responds with a smile.

Now I understand why he was hesitant to answer: he didn't want to offend me. I'm a pastor ... who does a lot of talking.

"I felt like I was *talking* about ministry in the midst of urgent spiritual and physical need," Aaron says, "more than I was *doing* ministry in the midst of urgent spiritual and physical need. And I decided that needed to change."

With these words we arrive at the airport. Aaron gives us instructions on how to go through the ticket counter and immigration in order to get to our flight on time. As he shakes hands with each of us, I realize that over the course of an unforgettable week, Aaron has become a good friend.

"Thank you, Aaron, for inviting me—and us—out here," I tell him. Wondering in the back of my mind if I might move here one day, I share, "I'm not sure how yet, but you can count on me—and us—being a part of this work in the days ahead."

He smiles, we hug, and we head off into the terminal.

As I'm about to board the plane, I know if I'm not careful, I can go home, and instead of leading my life and family and church with urgency, I can easily settle into complacency. But the Kamals and trafficked girls and people on the verge of being placed on funeral pyres don't need complacency. They don't need me and other Christians living as if somebody somewhere will do something someday about their urgent spiritual and physical needs. They need me and other Christians living as if this day could be their last.

Our plane is about to board. As I put my Bible and journal away, Chris asks, "David, how would you summarize your takeaway from this trip?"

I don't have to think long to respond. I know exactly what God has said to me through His Word during time in these mountains. "Something needs to change," I say. "In my life. In our families. In our church. I don't know exactly what that means, but I just know I can't—and we can't—continue with business as usual. Something needs to change now."

So what needs to change? I certainly don't presume to know the answer to that question for you. My primary aim in sharing this trek with you has been to bring you to the point—along with me—of asking the question. To the point where you feel, maybe in a fresh way in your heart, that Jesus is indeed the ultimate hope in a world of urgent need. And you realize that we each have unique opportunities to spread His hope amid the most hopeless situations in the world around us, no matter where we live.

One danger of trips like this is that we can experience various emotions and maybe even make various commitments, but within weeks of the return, our lives look just the way they did before we went. Obviously, this has been a Bible study and not a trip, but I wonder if the same danger is in play. And I really believe this study has missed the mark if your life ends up looking just the way it did before you completed it.

I've thought much about Proverbs 24:11-12 since I first encountered these mountains. God says:

> *Rescue those being taken off to death,*
> *and save those stumbling toward slaughter.*
> *If you say, "But we didn't know about this,"*
> *won't he who weighs hearts consider it?*
> *Won't he who protects your life know?*
> *Won't he repay a person according to his work?*

PROVERBS 24:11-12

In other words, you and I are accountable for what we know. I'm accountable for what I've seen in those mountains, and now that you've participated in this Bible study, you're accountable as well. If we know people are suffering both physically and spiritually, we're accountable before God for what we do or don't do in response.

Now that you know the needs and are accountable to respond, what is God putting on your heart to change in your life? How will you resist the status quo and complacency?

PERSONAL STUDY 1

READ

Slowly and intentionally read the Scriptures.

RREAD LUKE 9:57-62.

As we finish out our study together, we're going to consider the wholehearted urgency that comes with following Jesus.

■ CONTEXT

SETTING

Jesus was approached by potential followers while He was traveling from one place to another. In each case some well-intentioned people approached and declared their devotion to Him. However, when the same potential disciples heard the cost of devotion, they reconsidered their positions.

LUKE 9:57-58

⁵⁷ As they were **traveling on the road** someone said to him, "I will follow you wherever you go."
⁵⁸ Jesus told him, "Foxes have dens, and birds of the sky have nests, but **the Son of Man has no place to lay his head**."

■ THE FIRST LESSON

CHOOSE THE CROSS OVER COMFORT [VV. 57-58]

Although the first man who approached Jesus said, "I will follow you wherever you go" (v. 57), this man likely believed Jesus was just another teacher whose disciples followed them around and learned at their feet. He clearly hadn't counted on Jesus' response. Following Jesus is much more than an opportunity to come and learn. People who follow Jesus must live with an open hand and must be willing to let go of whatever keeps them from obeying Jesus.

■ THE SECOND LESSON

SACRIFICE FOR MISSION INSTEAD
OF SETTLING FOR MAINTENANCE [VV. 59-60]

In this second encounter Jesus approached a would-be disciple and extended a call to follow Him. The man responded by asking for a seemingly reasonable exception: he claimed that he needed to bury his father. In Jewish culture, burial of the dead was a religious duty to be attended to immediately. To leave this task unfinished would have been unthinkable. Jesus wasn't being callous; rather, He was underscoring the urgency of His calling. When Jesus calls us to follow Him, there's no time to maintain the status quo; there's no time for delay.

LUKE 9:59-62

59 Then he said to another, "Follow me."
"Lord," he said, **"first let me go bury my father."**
60 But he told him, "Let the dead bury their own dead, but you go and spread the news of the kingdom of God."
61 Another said, **"I will follow you, Lord, but first let me go and say good-bye to those at my house."**
62 But Jesus said to him, "No one who puts his hand to the plow and looks back is fit for the kingdom of God."

■ THE THIRD LESSON

BE MARKED BY AN UNDIVIDED HEART
INSTEAD OF AN INDECISIVE MIND [VV. 61-62]

Finally, another man approached Jesus and made another not-so-unreasonable request: to go and say goodbye to His family. After all, Elisha did this when he went with Elijah (see 1 Kings 19:20). However, following Jesus is a much more serious matter than following Elijah. Hidden in the request was reluctance that Jesus noticed. Disciples of Jesus must not be reluctant when He calls them forward.

EXAMINE

Gain a deeper appreciation for what the biblical text says.

What would you say is the major theme of all three interactions with Jesus?

What are we meant to learn from the fact that the requests of these would-be followers seemed entirely reasonable?

What similar excuses might a person make today?

APPLY

Recognize that the Bible calls us to obey God and to respond to Him with our lives.

In what areas of your life are you more prone to talk rather than act in living out your commitment to Jesus?

Is there anything Jesus is asking you to do for which you're presently making excuses? If so, what? Ask a group member or another Christian friend to pray that you'll overcome this hurdle.

PRAY

Respond to God with praise, thanksgiving, confession, and obedience.

Record a prayer to God in light of today's reading.

PERSONAL STUDY 2

READ

Slowly and intentionally read the Scriptures.

READ LUKE 16:19-31.

Today's reading highlights the urgency of pursuing Jesus. Hell is a stark reality for all who don't embrace Jesus as Savior and Lord. The reality of hell is described in more sobering detail in this passage than perhaps anywhere else in Scripture.

LUKE 16:19-24

19 "There was a **rich man** who would dress in purple and fine linen, feasting lavishly every day. 20 But a poor man named **Lazarus**, covered with sores, was lying at his gate. 21 He longed to be filled with what fell from the rich man's table, but instead the dogs would come and lick his sores. 22 One day the poor man died and was carried away by the angels to Abraham's side. The rich man also died and was buried. 23 And being in torment in Hades, he looked up and saw Abraham a long way off, with Lazarus at his side. 24 'Father Abraham!' he called out, 'Have mercy on me and send Lazarus to dip the tip of his finger in water and cool my tongue, because I am in agony in this flame!'

■ TWO CHARACTERS

THE RICH MAN [V. 19]

We get no name other than "a rich man" (v. 19). This rich man wasn't in hell simply because he was wealthy. Instead, he was in hell because he was a sinner whose heart indulged in his own luxuries while he ignored the poor. He knew they existed, but he did nothing to help them. His neglect of the poor demonstrated that His heart wasn't aligned with God's.

LAZARUS [V. 20]

The name Lazarus means "one whom God helps." Lazarus was obviously poor—sick and crippled, lying at the gates of the rich where he longed for food from the rich man's table as dogs licked his sores. God hears the cries of the poor and needy (see Job 34:28) and acts on their behalf, responding to their needs with compassion.

LUKE 16:25-31

25 " 'Son,' Abraham said, 'remember that during your life you received your good things, just as Lazarus received bad things, but now he is comforted here, while you are in agony. 26 Besides all this, a great **chasm has been fixed** between us and you, so that those who want to pass over from here to you cannot; neither can those from there cross over to us.'

27 " 'Father,' he said, 'then I beg you to send him to my father's house — 28 because I have five brothers — to warn them, so they won't also come to this place of torment.'

29 "But Abraham said, **'They have Moses and the prophets; they should listen to them.'**

30 " 'No, father Abraham,' he said. 'But if someone from the dead goes to them, they will repent.'

31 "But he told him, 'If they don't listen to Moses and the prophets, they will not be persuaded if someone rises from the dead.' "

ETERNITY

The language in this passage shows the finality of eternity. Upon death all people spend eternity in one of two places, heaven or hell. There are no other options or second chances; their destination is fixed. The urgency of eternity heightens the stakes in our calling to the nations.

■ ABRAHAM'S RESPONSE

Abraham's response to the rich man was tender, addressing him as "Son" (v. 25). In turn, the rich man begged that someone from the dead would go and warn his brothers about the coming judgment. Abraham asserted that the rich man and his brothers had a witness in the Scriptures that they found unconvincing. In other words, his unbelief came from a hard heart, not from a lack of evidence.

EXAMINE

Gain a deeper appreciation for what the biblical text says.

We know that salvation comes by faith, not by works. However, how did the rich man's actions reveal his heart?

What words and phrases are used to describe hell in this passage?

How does Luke 16:31 point to the continued rejection of Jesus in our own time?

APPLY

Recognize that the Bible calls us to obey God and to respond to Him with our lives.

How is the eternal reality of heaven and hell motivating you to live with urgency?

If the urgency of eternity isn't compelling you to share with unbelievers, what aren't you believing about the truth of the gospel?

Does your life match what you profess to believe? If not, what needs to change?

PRAY

Respond to God with praise, thanksgiving, confession, and obedience.

Record a prayer to God in light of today's reading.

PERSONAL STUDY 3

READ

Slowly and intentionally read the Scriptures.

READ LUKE 24:44-49.

These are the last words from Jesus in Luke's Gospel before He ascended to heaven. From them we receive crucial instructions about our mission as His followers.

■ CONTEXT

THE LAW OF MOSES, THE PROPHETS, AND THE PSALMS [V. 44]

Jesus used "the Law of Moses, the Prophets, and the Psalms" (v. 44) as shorthand to mean the entire Old Testament.

LUKE 24:44-45

⁴⁴ He told them, "These are my words that I spoke to you while I was still with you — that **everything written about me** in the Law of Moses, the Prophets, and the Psalms must be fulfilled." ⁴⁵ Then he opened their minds to understand the Scriptures.

■ JESUS IS THE KEY

The Scriptures tell one unified story about Jesus. Jesus emphasized this reality in John 5:39: "You pore over the Scriptures because you think you have eternal life in them, and yet they testify about me." All Scriptures, not just the Gospels or the New Testament, tell one story—creation, fall, redemption, and restoration—with Jesus at the center. Once we realize that all Scripture points to Jesus, we're better able to understand and respond to God's Word.

Hopefully, you've seen in this study how important Bible reading is for healthy spiritual development. To pursue Jesus, we must continually feed ourselves with the Scriptures.

■ GOD'S PLAN

Jesus' words reveal God's plan to His disciples. Jesus' suffering and death were part of God's plan from the beginning to restore the world. Through Jesus' death on the cross, God's wrath against sin was satisfied. All people who believe by grace through faith in Jesus' sacrifice on their behalf won't perish but will have everlasting life (see John 3:16).

LUKE 24:46-49

46 He also said to them, "This is what is written: The Messiah would suffer and rise from the dead the third day, 47 and repentance for forgiveness of sins would be proclaimed in his name to all the nations, beginning at Jerusalem. 48 You are **witnesses** of these things. 49 And look, I am sending you what my Father promised. As for you, stay in the city until you are **empowered from on high**."

■ WORD STUDY

WITNESSES [V. 48]

A witness (see Luke 24:48) is someone who can give an account of what they've seen, heard, or experienced. Thus, anyone who knows Jesus is a witness. Being a witness simply means you're able to tell someone about the God who saved you through Christ.

■ EMPOWERED FROM ON HIGH [V. 49]

As we seek to share the gospel, we should remember that God has sent us a Helper (see John 14:26) to empower us. Jesus' promise of the coming Holy Spirit was fulfilled in the Book of Acts, the sequel to Luke's Gospel. When Peter preached on Pentecost, the Holy Spirit descended and empowered the disciples to take the gospel to the nations (see Acts 2). All work to advance the gospel must be done in the power of the Spirit.

EXAMINE

Gain a deeper appreciation for what the biblical text says.

What elements of the gospel message did Jesus identify in His words to the disciples in Luke 24:44-49?

How does Jesus make sense of the entire Bible?

In what ways are all believers witnesses to the work of Christ even though we're centuries removed from the first disciples?

APPLY

Recognize that the Bible calls us to obey God and to respond to Him with our lives.

How can you rely more on the Holy Spirit as you seek to make Christ known among all nations?

What are the most significant obstacles to your living with urgency for people in need around you, as well as for people around the world?

What needs to change in your own life?

PRAY

Respond to God with praise, thanksgiving, confession, and obedience.

Record a prayer to God in light of today's reading.

PARTICIPANT GUIDE

■ HOW TO USE THIS PARTICIPANT GUIDE

Each session of *Something Needs to Change* Bible study includes a participant guide to help you follow along with the video teaching and think about the content throughout the week.

Each page is designed to be cut out and used by participants in the group. The front side is meant to be used during the group session, while the back side is meant to be used for personal study and application between group sessions.

If all participants don't have Bible-study books, copies of the participant guide are available at LifeWay.com/SomethingNeedstoChange.

■ SCRIPTURE

This section provides the Scripture passage David taught during the video session.

■ TEACHING POINTS

This section lists primary points contained in David's teaching.

■ ACTION STEPS

This study calls you to make a difference as you live your life. Each session provides several key action steps you could take to live out key teachings presented in this study.

■ QUESTIONS TO CONSIDER

Several questions are provided to help you think more deeply about the issues being discussed in the group sessions. The purpose of these questions is for you to evaluate your heart and allow the gospel to transform your heart, mind, and actions.

SESSION 1: REPENTANCE

Use this page to follow along with the video teaching.

■ SCRIPTURE

In the fifteenth year of the reign of Tiberius Caesar, while Pontius Pilate was governor of Judea, Herod was tetrarch of Galilee, his brother Philip tetrarch of the region of Iturea and Trachonitis, and Lysanias tetrarch of Abilene, during the high priesthood of Annas and Caiaphas, God's word came to John the son of Zechariah in the wilderness. He went into all the vicinity of the Jordan, proclaiming a baptism of repentance for the forgiveness of sins, as it is written in the book of the words of the prophet Isaiah: "A voice of one crying out in the wilderness: Prepare the way for the Lord; make his paths straight! Every valley will be filled, and every mountain and hill will be made low; the crooked will become straight, the rough ways smooth, and everyone will see the salvation of God." He then said to the crowds who came out to be baptized by him, "Brood of vipers! Who warned you to flee from the coming wrath? Therefore produce fruit consistent with repentance. And don't start saying to yourselves, 'We have Abraham as our father,' for I tell you that God is able to raise up children for Abraham from these stones. The ax is already at the root of the trees. Therefore, every tree that doesn't produce good fruit will be cut down and thrown into the fire." "What then should we do?" the crowds were asking him. He replied to them, "The one who has two shirts must share with someone who has none, and the one who has food must do the same." Tax collectors also came to be baptized, and they asked him, "Teacher, what should we do?" He told them, "Don't collect any more than what you have been authorized." Some soldiers also questioned him, "What should we do?" He said to them, "Don't take money from anyone by force or false accusation, and be satisfied with your wages." Now the people were waiting expectantly, and all of them were questioning in their hearts whether John might be the Messiah. John answered them all, "I baptize you with water, but one who is more powerful than I am is coming. I am not worthy to untie the strap of his sandals. He will baptize you with the Holy Spirit and fire. His winnowing shovel is in his hand to clear his threshing floor and gather the wheat into his barn, but the chaff he will burn with fire that never goes out." Then, along with many other exhortations, he proclaimed good news to the people.

LUKE 3:1-18

■ TEACHING POINTS

It is dangerously possible to have religion without repentance.

It is completely impossible to be a Christian without change.

Judgment is inevitable for every person, based upon how they respond to Jesus.

Hope is available to all people because of the good news of Jesus.

■ STEPS TO TAKE

Consider the following suggestions for becoming involved in God's work in your community and around the world.

Meet with a trusted Christian friend and identify areas of your life in which your actions don't line up with what you profess to believe.

Make a list of places you've been or experiences you've had in which you personally encountered urgent spiritual and physical needs. What lasting effect(s) did those experiences have?

Use JoshuaProject.org, OpenDoorsUSA.org, PeopleGroups.org, and other resources to learn about some of the most urgent needs among unreached people groups and in places where the church is persecuted.

■ QUESTIONS TO CONSIDER

Use these questions to consider and apply what you've learned in this session over the next week. We'll talk about them at our next group session.

Who's a leader or a friend at your church you could connect with to identify ways to join Christ's work through your local body of believers?

What are you learning about repentance? Why should repentance be an ongoing component of the Christian life?

Who in your life needs to hear the gospel and believe in Jesus? Spend a few minutes asking God to convict you of the need to reach a person or a people group, like those in the Himalayas, who need the gospel. Then pray that He will use you to take His hope to them.

SESSION 2: PHYSICAL NEED

Use this page to follow along with the video teaching.

■ SCRIPTURE

He came to Nazareth, where he had been brought up. As usual, he entered the synagogue on the Sabbath day and stood up to read. The scroll of the prophet Isaiah was given to him, and unrolling the scroll, he found the place where it was written: "The Spirit of the Lord is on me, because he has anointed me to preach good news to the poor. He has sent me to proclaim release to the captives and recovery of sight to the blind, to set free the oppressed, to proclaim the year of the Lord's favor." He then rolled up the scroll, gave it back to the attendant, and sat down. And the eyes of everyone in the synagogue were fixed on him. He began by saying to them, "Today as you listen, this Scripture has been fulfilled."

LUKE 4:16-21

While he was in one of the towns, a man was there who had leprosy all over him. He saw Jesus, fell facedown, and begged him: "Lord, if you are willing, you can make me clean." Reaching out his hand, Jesus touched him, saying, "I am willing; be made clean," and immediately the leprosy left him. Then he ordered him to tell no one: "But go and show yourself to the priest, and offer what Moses commanded for your cleansing as a testimony to them." But the news about him spread even more, and large crowds would come together to hear him and to be healed of their sicknesses.

LUKE 5:12-15

■ TEACHING POINTS

How should you and I live in a world of urgent physical need?

We don't turn from need. We run to need.

■ ACTION STEPS

Consider the following suggestions for becoming involved in God's work in your community and around the world.

Meet with a pastor or church leader to discover information about ways your church is serving your city by meeting spiritual and physical needs.

Do you feel a particular passion for any needs, such as homelessness, orphan care, or victims of abuse? Find out where God is meeting those needs in your city.

What are some physical needs that exist around the world? Brainstorm ways to raise material resources to alleviate this suffering.

Identify at least one way you, your family, or your friends could sacrificially meet a need in your community. Make a specific plan to meet this need and set a timetable. Pray that God will use your efforts to draw attention to Himself and that your efforts will provide an opportunity to share the gospel.

■ QUESTIONS TO CONSIDER

Use these questions to consider and apply what you've learned in this session over the next week. We'll talk about them at our next group session.

We don't have to go to the other side of the world to meet urgent physical need. What are a few ways God can use you to meet physical need where you are?

In what ways is your local church currently running to need? How could you be involved?

Spend time asking God to help you identify areas of apathy and indifference in your life. Pray that God, through His Spirit, will create a burden in you to meet the needs around you in Jesus' name.

SESSION 3: SPIRITUAL NEED

Use this page to follow along with the video teaching.

■ SCRIPTURE

On one of those days while he was teaching, Pharisees and teachers of the law were sitting there who had come from every village of Galilee and Judea, and also from Jerusalem. And the Lord's power to heal was in him. Just then some men came, carrying on a stretcher a man who was paralyzed. They tried to bring him in and set him down before him. Since they could not find a way to bring him in because of the crowd, they went up on the roof and lowered him on the stretcher through the roof tiles into the middle of the crowd before Jesus. Seeing their faith he said, "Friend, your sins are forgiven." Then the scribes and the Pharisees began to think to themselves: "Who is this man who speaks blasphemies? Who can forgive sins but God alone?" But perceiving their thoughts, Jesus replied to them, "Why are you thinking this in your hearts? Which is easier: to say, 'Your sins are forgiven,' or to say, 'Get up and walk'? But so that you may know that the Son of Man has authority on earth to forgive sins"—he told the paralyzed man, "I tell you: Get up, take your stretcher, and go home." Immediately he got up before them, picked up what he had been lying on, and went home glorifying God. Then everyone was astounded, and they were giving glory to God. And they were filled with awe and said, "We have seen incredible things today."

LUKE 5:17-26

■ ACTION STEPS

Consider the following suggestions for becoming involved in God's work in your community and around the world.

David stated that many Christians don't feel comfortable sharing the gospel. Compose a gospel presentation and think about a way you could communicate that message to another person. Practice sharing what you've recorded with a friend and ask for feedback.

Cultivate relationships with people who haven't yet believed in Jesus.

Identify at least one unbeliever among your family, friends, coworkers, or neighbors for whom you'll pray and with whom you'll attempt to share the gospel over the next month. Ask another church member to pray for you.

■ QUESTIONS TO CONSIDER

Use these questions to consider and apply what you've learned in this session over the next week. We'll talk about them at our next group session.

If we truly believe that people who die without knowing Jesus spend an eternity apart from God in hell, why do we live with so little urgency? How could you live more intentionally for the sake of those who haven't believed?

What changes do you need to make in your life in order to respond to spiritual need around you?

SESSION 4: LOVING GOD AND OTHERS

Use this page to follow along with the video teaching.

■ SCRIPTURE

An expert in the law stood up to test him, saying, "Teacher, what must I do to inherit eternal life?" "What is written in the law?" he asked him. "How do you read it?" He answered, "Love the Lord your God with all your heart, with all your soul, with all your strength, and with all your mind," and "your neighbor as yourself." "You've answered correctly," he told him. "Do this and you will live." But wanting to justify himself, he asked Jesus, "And who is my neighbor?" Jesus took up the question and said: "A man was going down from Jerusalem to Jericho and fell into the hands of robbers. They stripped him, beat him up, and fled, leaving him half dead." A priest happened to be going down that road. When he saw him, he passed by on the other side. In the same way, a Levite, when he arrived at the place and saw him, passed by on the other side. But a Samaritan on his journey came up to him, and when he saw the man, he had compassion. He went over to him and bandaged his wounds, pouring on olive oil and wine. Then he put him on his own animal, brought him to an inn, and took care of him. The next day he took out two denarii, gave them to the innkeeper, and said, "Take care of him. When I come back I'll reimburse you for whatever extra you spend." Which of these three do you think proved to be a neighbor to the man who fell into the hands of the robbers? "The one who showed mercy to him," he said. Then Jesus told him, "Go and do the same."

LUKE 10:25-37

■ ACTION STEPS

Consider the following suggestions for becoming involved in God's work in your community and around the world.

Find local organizations that are committed to meet physical needs in order to meet spiritual needs. Find ways to partner with them as a way of loving God and others.

Identify a need in your church that you could address, such as sending money or a care package to a missionary, visiting a homebound member, preparing a meal for someone who's in the hospital, or offering to pray with someone who's suffering.

■ QUESTIONS TO CONSIDER

Use these questions to consider and apply what you've learned in this session over the next week. We'll talk about them at our next group session.

What small (even good) practices and pursuits do you or does your church focus on that keep you from concentrating on the most important priorities?

Sometime during the next week, meet with a friend from church to talk about ways you could show unselfish love to your community, to confess where you've failed, and to pray for God to use your church in your community. Record some reflections from that conversation.

SESSION 5: OPPORTUNITIES

Use this page to follow along with the video teaching.

◼ SCRIPTURE

He told them a parable: "A rich man's land was very productive. He thought to himself, 'What should I do, since I don't have anywhere to store my crops? I will do this,' he said. 'I'll tear down my barns and build bigger ones and store all my grain and my goods there. Then I'll say to myself, "You have many goods stored up for many years. Take it easy; eat, drink, and enjoy yourself." ' But God said to him, 'You fool! This very night your life is demanded of you. And the things you have prepared—whose will they be?' That's how it is with the one who stores up treasure for himself and is not rich toward God."

LUKE 12:16-21

Don't be afraid, little flock, because your Father delights to give you the kingdom. Sell your possessions and give to the poor. Make money-bags for yourselves that won't grow old, an inexhaustible treasure in heaven, where no thief comes near and no moth destroys. For where your treasure is, there your heart will be also.

LUKE 12:32-34

The Lord said: "Who then is the faithful and sensible manager his master will put in charge of his household servants to give them their allotted food at the proper time? Blessed is that servant whom the master finds doing his job when he comes. Truly I tell you, he will put him in charge of all his possessions. But if that servant says in his heart, 'My master is delaying his coming,' and starts to beat the male and female servants, and to eat and drink and get drunk, that servant's master will come on a day he does not expect him and at an hour he does not know. He will cut him to pieces and assign him a place with the unfaithful. And that servant who knew his master's will and didn't prepare himself or do it will be severely beaten. But the one who did not know and did what deserved punishment will receive a light beating. From everyone who has been given much, much will be required; and from the one who has been entrusted with much, even more will be expected."

LUKE 12:42-48

◼ TEACHING POINTS

The life that counts is rich toward God and generous toward others.

The life that counts gives generously because it rests continually in God's love.

The life that counts turns much grace from God into much glory for God.

■ ACTION STEPS

Consider the following suggestions for becoming involved in God's work in your community and around the world.

Find other believers in your workplace or in your vocation. Think together about ways you can use your profession or skills for the kingdom of God.

Connect with a minister at your church and discover ways your gifts can be used on a short-term mission trip.

■ QUESTIONS TO CONSIDER

Use these questions to consider and apply what you've learned in this session over the next week. We'll talk about them at our next group session.

"From everyone who has been given much, much will be required; and from the one who has been entrusted with much, even more will be expected" (Luke 12:48). What comes to your mind when you read this verse?

What might God require from you, based on what He has given you? Spend a few moments praying about this question before recording your answer.

How could you use the unique gifts God has given you in places far away from where you live?

SESSION 6: THE COST

Use this page to follow along with the video teaching.

■ SCRIPTURE

Great crowds were traveling with him. So he turned and said to them: "If anyone comes to me and does not hate his own father and mother, wife and children, brothers and sisters—yes, and even his own life—he cannot be my disciple. Whoever does not bear his own cross and come after me cannot be my disciple. For which of you, wanting to build a tower, doesn't first sit down and calculate the cost to see if he has enough to complete it? Otherwise, after he has laid the foundation and cannot finish it, all the onlookers will begin to ridicule him, saying, 'This man started to build and wasn't able to finish.' Or what king, going to war against another king, will not first sit down and decide if he is able with ten thousand to oppose the one who comes against him with twenty thousand? If not, while the other is still far off, he sends a delegation and asks for terms of peace. In the same way, therefore, every one of you who does not renounce all his possessions cannot be my disciple."

LUKE 14:25-33

■ TEACHING POINTS

Jesus requires superior love.

Jesus requires exclusive loyalty.

Jesus requires total loss.

Jesus is supremely loving.

Jesus is supremely loyal.

Jesus suffered the ultimate loss.

■ ACTION STEPS

Consider the following suggestions for becoming involved in God's work in your community and around the world.

Two billion people don't have access to the knowledge that Jesus can save them from their sins. What resources could you sacrifice to make sure the gospel reaches them?

Talk to a church leader and investigate ways you can support the persecuted church through praying, giving, and going.

■ QUESTIONS TO CONSIDER

Use these questions to consider and apply what you've learned in this session over the next week. We'll talk about them at our next group session.

What is it costing you to follow Jesus in your life right now? If it isn't costing you something, why isn't it?

What steps of obedience to Jesus might make following Him most costly?

Over the next several days find a time to meet with someone from this group or someone else from your church. Spend concentrated time praying and asking Jesus to help you boldly pursue Him no matter the cost. Record some reflections on this concentrated time of prayer.

SESSION 7: THE ONE

Use this page to follow along with the video teaching.

■ SCRIPTURE

All the tax collectors and sinners were approaching to listen to him. And the Pharisees and scribes were complaining, "This man welcomes sinners and eats with them." So he told them this parable: "What man among you, who has a hundred sheep and loses one of them, does not leave the ninety-nine in the open field and go after the lost one until he finds it? When he has found it, he joyfully puts it on his shoulders, and coming home, he calls his friends and neighbors together, saying to them, 'Rejoice with me, because I have found my lost sheep!' I tell you, in the same way, there will be more joy in heaven over one sinner who repents than over ninety-nine righteous people who don't need repentance. Or what woman who has ten silver coins, if she loses one coin, does not light a lamp, sweep the house, and search carefully until she finds it? When she finds it, she calls her friends and neighbors together, saying, 'Rejoice with me, because I have found the silver coin I lost!' I tell you, in the same way, there is joy in the presence of God's angels over one sinner who repents." He also said: "A man had two sons. The younger of them said to his father, 'Father, give me the share of the estate I have coming to me.' So he distributed the assets to them. Not many days later, the younger son gathered together all he had and traveled to a distant country, where he squandered his estate in foolish living. After he had spent everything, a severe famine struck that country, and he had nothing. Then he went to work for one of the citizens of that country, who sent him into his fields to feed pigs. He longed to eat his fill from the pods that the pigs were eating, but no one would give him anything. When he came to his senses, he said, 'How many of my father's hired workers have more than enough food, and here I am dying of hunger! I'll get up, go to my father, and say to him, "Father, I have sinned against heaven and in your sight. I'm no longer worthy to be called your son. Make me like one of your hired workers." ' So he got up and went to his father. But while the son was still a long way off, his father saw him and was filled with compassion. He ran, threw his arms around his neck, and kissed him. The son said to him, 'Father, I have sinned against heaven and in your sight. I'm no longer worthy to be called your son.' But the father told his servants, 'Quick! Bring out the best robe and put it on him; put a ring on his finger and sandals on his feet. Then bring the fattened calf and slaughter it, and let's celebrate with a feast, because this son of mine was dead and is alive again; he was lost and is found!' So they began to celebrate. Now his older son was in the field; as he came near the house, he heard music and dancing. So he summoned one of the servants, questioning what these things meant. 'Your brother is here,' he told him, 'and your father has slaughtered the fattened calf because he has him back safe and sound.' Then he became angry and didn't want to go in. So his father came out and pleaded with him. But he replied to his father, 'Look, I have been slaving many years for you, and I have never disobeyed your orders, yet you never gave me a goat so that I could celebrate with my friends. But when this son of yours came, who has devoured your assets with prostitutes, you slaughtered the fattened calf for him.' 'Son,' he said to him, 'you are always with me, and everything I have is yours. But we had to celebrate and rejoice, because this brother of yours was dead and is alive again; he was lost and is found.' "

LUKE 15

■ ACTION STEPS

Consider the following suggestions for becoming involved in God's work in your community and around the world.

Identify one person you know who has yet to believe the gospel. Commit to pray for them daily and to spend time with them regularly.

Learn the names of missionaries your church supports on the field. Connect with them and discover specific needs you can meet through praying, giving, and going to serve them.

■ QUESTIONS TO CONSIDER

Use these questions to consider and apply what you've learned in this session over the next week. We'll talk about them at our next group session.

Who's one person you're praying for in the hope that they'll come to a saving knowledge of Jesus Christ?

Do you spend any time with people who haven't yet believed? If not, in what areas of your schedule can you make time to intentionally befriend and care for those in your community who don't know Jesus?

Spend time in prayer asking God to give you grace and opportunities with a lost friend. Pray that He will give you boldness and confidence as you seek to care for this person and share the gospel.

SESSION 8: SOMETHING NEEDS TO CHANGE

Use this page to follow along with the video teaching.

■ SCRIPTURE

As they were traveling on the road someone said to him, "I will follow you wherever you go." Jesus told him, "Foxes have dens, and birds of the sky have nests, but the Son of Man has no place to lay his head." Then he said to another, "Follow me." "Lord," he said, "first let me go bury my father." But he told him, "Let the dead bury their own dead, but you go and spread the news of the kingdom of God." Another said, "I will follow you, Lord, but first let me go and say good-bye to those at my house." But Jesus said to him, "No one who puts his hand to the plow and looks back is fit for the kingdom of God."

LUKE 9:57-62

In the same way, when you have done all that you were commanded, you should say, "We are worthless servants; we've only done our duty."

LUKE 17:10

■ TEACHING POINTS

Are you going to choose comfort, or are you going to choose the cross?

Are you going to settle for maintenance, or are you going to sacrifice for mission?

Will your life be marked by an indecisive mind or an undivided heart?

Work hard to help well amidst earthly suffering.

Work hardest to keep people from eternal suffering.

Be the church God calls us to be.

Run the race God calls you to run.

■ ACTION STEPS

Consider the following suggestions for becoming involved in God's work in your community and around the world.

Look at your budget. Consider ways you could reduce unessential expenses in order to leverage your resources for the advancement of God's kingdom.

■ QUESTIONS TO CONSIDER

Use these questions to consider and apply what you've learned throughout this study.

Are you going to choose comfort, or are you going to choose the cross?
What comforts is God calling you to forsake in order to embrace the cross?

Are you going to settle for maintenance, or are you going to sacrifice for mission?
What sacrifices do you need to make?

Will your life be marked by an indecisive mind or an undivided heart?
What needs to change in your life?

If you judge a journey by how different you are upon your return, David Platt experienced the trip of a lifetime.

Something Needs to Change is a raw, irresistible message about what it means to stop talking about faith and start living it, right where you are.

Start reading at Radical.net/SomethingNeedsToChange

MULTNOMAH

WHERE TO GO FROM HERE

We hope you were challenged and inspired by *Something Needs to Change*. Now that you've completed this study, here are a few possible directions you can go for your next one.

OBEY GOD & DENY SELF

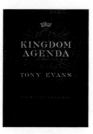

KINGDOM AGENDA
Tony Evans

Learn to apply biblical kingdom principles to everyday realities for the individual, the family, the church, or the nation. (6 sessions)

ENGAGE WITH SCRIPTURE

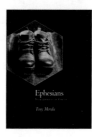

EPHESIANS
Tony Merida

Challenge the status quo of our culture (and even some churches) by encouraging your group to live the essential convictions of Christianity more purely. (6 sessions)

SHARE CHRIST

SHARE JESUS WITHOUT FEAR
William Fay, Ralph Hodge

Begin using a simple and relational approach to witnessing that underscores the dependence on God's power for the results. (4 sessions)

EXERCISE FAITH

RECOVERING REDEMPTION
Matt Chandler

Discover the antidote to sin and suffering in this broken world by recovering a right understanding of the gospel and learning how to live it out. (12 sessions)

More from
DAVID PLATT

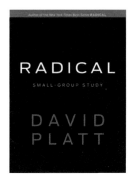

RADICAL | lifeway.com/radical
6 sessions

Discover what Jesus actually said about being His disciple,
and see what happens when you begin to obey.

Leader Kit 005471377
Bible Study Book 005471378

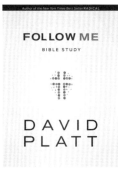

FOLLOW ME | lifeway.com/followme
6 sessions

Challenge the traditions of cultural Christianity, and examine
the meaning of Jesus' simple request: Follow Me.

Bible Study Book with Video Access 005839412
Bible Study eBook with Video Access 005839413

COUNTER CULTURE | lifeway.com/counterculture
6 sessions

See how the gospel compels followers of Christ to counter culture
on a wide variety of social issues in the world around them.

Leader Kit 005703479
Bible Study Book 005703478

LEARN MORE ONLINE OR CALL 800.458.2772

Thousands of gospel-equipping resources—
now more accessible than ever.

EXPLORE
RADICAL.NET